# Have a look at the fastest sprea... RUMOR in town

KARAT TOP METAKON

ALUKON

AND *Thunderbird* TRADEMARK

# coats · suits

1. Middy-suit by Chantelle is young and vivacious fine wool with swinging sunray skirt. Price £7 7s. 4d.

2. Rich silk grosgrain livens Penny Mason's unlined pastel wool suit at £4 6s. 9d. ● 3. The oblique fastening and half-cuffed sleeves make Dereta's jacket in peacock velour an exciting "buy" at £9. Black toothpick skirt is £2 12s. 6d. ● 4. Seton Cotterill's town or country suit in hardwearing, blended pastel tweed boasts a box-pleated, freedom skirt, costs £10 11s. 4d. ● 5. Revel in grey flannel, spring's first love, with Harella's tailored topcoat at £7 11s. ● 6. Or frame your face dramatically in tweed with Paneth's double Medici collar. This coat is 9 gns., with grey suit at same price. ●

# The 1950s Look

## A Practical Guide to Fashions, Hairstyles and Make-up of the 1950s

First published in the United Kingdom in 2008
by Sabrestorm Publishing
90, Lennard Road, Dunton Green,
Sevenoaks, Kent TN13 2UX

www.sabrestorm.com

British Library Cataloguing in Publication Data
A catalogue record for this book is available from the British Library.

Designed and typeset by Annie Falconer-Gronow

ISBN: 978-0-9552723-3-2

Printed by Tien Wah Press

# The 1950s Look

A Practical Guide to Fashions, Hairstyles and Make-up of the 1950s

## Mike Brown

SABRESTORM

# *Thanks*

I would like to take this opportunity to thank the following people; Emilie Boudette, for typing help, the College of Optometrists, and especially their librarian, Ms. Carrie Sherlock. Our designer Annie Falconer-Gronow, my publisher Ian Bayley, and as ever, our families, Jan, Michael and Charlotte, and Carol, William and Ralph.

# CONTENTS

# CLOTHING

## *Introduction*

**1945** not only brought the end of the Second World War but was in many ways the start of a new world. On VJ Day, King George VI had broadcast to the nation: *'We have our part to play in restoring the shattered fabric of civilisation. . . . It is to this great task that I call you now, and I know that I shall not call in vain.'*

Clement Attlee's new Labour government was convinced that the methods by which the war had been won could also help to 'win the peace'. Wartime production methods, which had seen the output of munitions and arms soar, could be used to manufacture the country out of debt, in combination with the tight central control of public consumption wielded by the Ministry of Food and the Board of Trade through rationing. Thus the end of the war did not, as many had hoped, mean the end of rationing. Indeed, some food would continue to be rationed until 1954: sweets until 1953, petrol until 1950 and furniture until 1948. And, of course, clothes rationing continued, even more strictly than during the war. In September 1945, one month after the end of the war, the clothing ration was cut to thirty-six coupons a year for an adult.

In 1946 the Council of Industrial Design put on an exhibition at the Victoria & Albert Museum, London, entitled 'Britain

▲ Catalogue from the 'Britain Can Make It' exhibition of 1946, rechristened by some 'Britain Can't Have It'.

Can Make It'. The fashion section featured the latest designs of the Incorporated Society of London Fashion Designers. As part of the government's austerity drive, these clothes were for export only, and so the fashion shows were put on a week before the Paris collections. The drive was surprisingly successful; export sales of British fashions rose from £98,000 in 1938 to £507,000 in 1946. Being for export only, some humorists changed the name from 'Britain Can Make It' to 'Britain Can't Have It'. It would be some years before any benefit of this resurgence of the British fashion scene was felt in the home market, where clothes remained strictly rationed and only Utility styles were available.

In 1947 the fashion world had been stunned by Christian Dior's first spring collection in which he showed dresses with nipped-in waists, heavy pleats and very full skirts. The overall effect was to create soft, rounded lines that were in complete contrast to the hard, austere look of the war years. Later Dior described the dresses that 'took up a fantastic yardage of material and this time went right down to the ankles. Girls could safely feel they had all the trappings of a fairytale princess to wear. A golden age seemed to have come again. War had passed out of sight, and there were no other wars on the horizon. What did the weight of my sumptuous materials, my heavy velvets and brocade matter? When hearts were light, mere fabrics could not weigh the body down.'

In Britain, as in France, there was at first an outcry over the extravagance of a garment that required 25 yards of material and new foundations that were then classed as 'luxury garments'. The president of the Board of Trade, Sir Stafford Cripps, wanted to outlaw such flagrant waste, but the look appealed to British women, starved as they were of glamour, and within the year the 'New Look' had spread across the country. Harold Wilson, who that year became Cripps' successor, was more stoical, commenting that 'If women are going to buy these skirts, they are going to have to buy fewer of them.' Responding to this wave of interest, British manufacturers were quick to bring out their own versions of the New Look.

At last, in March 1948, Wilson announced the relaxation of the rationing system, and in February 1949 it was declared that clothes rationing would cease one month later, with many garments becoming coupon-free immediately. The Utility scheme continued to operate, controlling the price and quality of garments for people of all ages, but it was a far cry from the all-embracing scheme that was running at the height of the war. Utility involved fewer and fewer restrictions until the scheme was finally wound up in 1952, by which time it was applied to a few items of clothing that were exempt from Purchase Tax but which few wanted.

◀ One of the dresses from Dior's 'New Look' range of 1947.

▶▶ A picture from 1950, which might easily be from 1940 or even 1930.

▶ Cold-weather wear – trilby hat, large overcoat, knitted scarf and gloves and, of course, the almost compulsory pipe – 1951.

# Men

*'No man in the world is so sordidly shabby as the Englishman on the beach (or in an office) on a hot day.'*
Cecil Beaton

It was perhaps in the area of men's clothing that the greatest changes took place in the 1950s. The beginning of the decade saw men wearing virtually the same type of clothes that they had worn ten years before: the lounge suit over a shirt and tie, often with a pullover, probably in Fair Isle, substituted for the waistcoat at weekends. The whole thing was topped off by a large overcoat, or a raincoat, and a trilby-type hat or flat cap.

Behind this, however, was brewing a quiet revolution. Conscription, followed by several years in uniform, during which time any laxness in dress could land you in trouble with the sergeant major, led to an increasing desire for less uniformity and a more casual approach to dress. This was helped along by an American influence. The war years saw the USA become the source of fashion, as the old continental centres dried up under German occupation. In the age of austerity, the USA represented everything that had disappeared in Britain; even the uniforms of the GIs, with their 'Ike jackets', looked so much better than the sack-like British battledress.

In the post-war period those who could get hold of them sported highly decorative, hand-painted ties featuring exotic scenes, skyscrapers, large jazzy patterns or flowers and, most daring of all, pin-up girls, the latter often appearing on the inside of the tie. When Cecil Gee in the Charing Cross Road started to import American men's clothing in 1946 queues formed outside. Another popular American import was the wide-shouldered 'Zoot suit'. Even before the war the fashion in British men's jackets had been for tightness and shortness and compared with the demob suit sported by so many ex-servicemen, the Zoot suit now seemed positively opulent. With its extra length, its roomy cut and its large, loud checks, it would remain the main influence on men's jackets in Britain, although usually in a somewhat subdued way, until the middle of the decade. This new style for men was dubbed the 'Bold Look' as opposed to their wives' 'New Look'.

The biggest revolution came in the guise of men's shirts. This began with the arrival of the Hawaiian shirt in the late 1940s. Another American import, the Hawaiian shirt was loose fitting, short sleeved, with an unbuttoned neck made to be worn without a tie. Even more revolutionary were its short, square-cut tails, designed to be worn outside the trousers. Like the American ties, these shirts were often brightly coloured and sported bold patterns. Afterwards came the Chat Way shirt, again open-necked but with three-quarter-length sleeves and, like the Hawaiian shirt, made to be worn outside the trousers. For this reason it had two front, hip-level pockets, thus becoming a cross between a shirt and a jacket, or, as similar shirts would later be called, a shirt-jacket.

As with women's clothes, the greatest innovation in men's clothing was the rapid expansion of the use of man-made fabrics. Their natural conservatism in clothes meant new ideas often took far longer to filter through into the average man's wardrobe, but these fabrics were different. This was something men could relate to — it was science, it was technology. Thus, many men welcomed the new materials — nylon, Terylene, Acrilan and an ever-increasing list of new textiles — with open arms. This was the new, scientific age of crease-resistant, drip-dry and permanent creased clothes. By the mid-1950s synthetic fabrics took up a significant part of most men's wardrobes, with many items of clothing, especially leisurewear and underwear, either completely synthetic or synthetic/wool or cotton blends. The use of these mixtures for what were called ventilated fabrics meant that suits became lighter to wear and looked less baggy and creased. They were further improved by the use of half-linings, otherwise known as English linings. **Men Only** magazine, November 1955, reported that: *'Average suit weights are gradually getting lighter. A cloth of 16-ozs-a-yard, once "normal", is now being reckoned a bit heavy; I'd settle for 14½-15ozs.'*

A letter to **Men Only**, July 1958, asked: *'When all the new "miracle" synthetic fibres began coming on the market we were told that the completely washable lounge suit was just around the corner. Is it, in fact, still "around the corner" whether near or far? Or has it happened and I've missed it?'*

The reply was: *'It depends on what you mean by the term "lounge suit". There's no problem at all in producing, say, an all-Terylene spun suiting which would have an appearance suitable for town clothes and which, in itself, would be washable. But if you then incorporate into a suit of such material all the normal types of interlining, padding, and tailor's trimmings generally, the suit would no longer be in the truly washable class. With unlined lightweights and suits of "tropical" type there is no such problem and the new washability is a reality. For normal lounge suits it is usually considered better to combine the synthetic yarn with wool or worsted, and to forgo the washability in favour of other all-round advantages.'* As early as 1951, the Ealing comedy, **The Man in the White Suit,** poked gentle fun at the new fabrics.

▶ Cartoon from **Men Only** magazine, April 1952. Ties with hand-painted pin-up girls were fashionable, if somewhat risqué.

"My wife asked me to exchange this for me."

American society was far less formal than Britain's in the post-war years, and this was reflected in American men's clothing, for example, the tie-less Hawaiian shirt and the growing market in denim jeans, driven initially by teenagers but slowly moving up the age ladder. The popularity of these fashions in Britain reflected not only the idea of America as the source of all things new and desirable in post-war Britain, but it also chimed neatly with Britain's growing wealth. Increasing wages meant not only more disposable income to spend on clothes, but also increased leisure time, for which the casual American styles were perfect. **Woman's Weekly**, January 1952, reported that: *'Many of our readers are becoming devotees of square dancing, which is such good fun. The costumes worn for these dances are characteristic. Gay plaid shirts and jeans for the men; cotton blouses and full skirts for the girls.'* Another new American-inspired leisure activity was ten-pin bowling, which brought with it the bowling shirt, another variation on the Hawaiian shirt.

But transatlantic fashions did not have it all their own way. Many men in Britain resented the American influence; they still remembered how difficult it had been for British men, troops or civilians, to get near British girls when the GIs were about with their plentiful money, nylons, sweets and other luxuries. While some were content to emulate the Americans, others wanted a purely British look. They looked back to an earlier time, the Edwardian period, when Britain really was Great and the leader of the western world. The nostalgia behind the New Look for women could also apply to men's fashions. Some upper-class officer types began to sport clothes similar to those their fathers, or grandfathers, had worn. This look comprised a long, plain, single-breasted, usually navy or black jacket with narrow lapels and narrow, pin-stripe trousers, all worn under a fitted 'City' coat of Crombie wool with a velvet collar, a descendant of the Edwardian frock coat, worn with a plain, double-breasted

▲ Bill Haley and the Comets. Their song *'Rock Around the Clock'* in the film **The Blackboard Jungle** had British teenagers dancing in the cinema aisles.

▲ The plaid sports shirt, 1952. As the advert says, they were very popular among square-dance enthusiasts – no rock and roll yet!

▼ A sporty zip-fronted knitted windcheater with the inevitable cravat, 1953.

waistcoat with wide (often rounded) lapels, a curly brimmed bowler hat and the almost compulsory umbrella. Little did these very upper-crust Britons know that they would inspire a group of south London teenagers to evolve into something of which they would most certainly not approve – the 'Edwardian' or 'Teddy' boys.

By the mid-1950s the general mood was changing. Men wanted new clothes, but they also wanted something more stylish, and the focus of men's fashion swung from America to Italy. Here a vibrant clothing industry was blossoming, based on modern styles but also on the idea of '*fare la bella figura*' – present-

ing a fine figure. Naples, Milan and Rome became the centres of the Italian menswear industry. British tourists, of whom there were an increasing number due to the combination of rising wages and falling travel costs, brought back sharp Italian suits and other clothes. The Italian fashion industry, benefiting as it did from low wages, reorganised itself to cater for the ever-growing ready-to-wear market.

An Italian suit became almost a status symbol. They differed from what had come before in many respects: they had a short 'Roman' jacket, harking back to the pre-war 'bum-freezer', which was short enough for the wearer to ride a Vespa or Lambretta scooter (another great Italian innovation of the period) without the jacket touching the seat, thereby keeping both their line and the rider's dignity. They had wide, square-cut, padded shoulders, and, again in contrast to the generous cut of previous suits, close-fitting, tapered trousers without pleats, worn with pointed 'winkle-picker' shoes or loafers. All of this might be worn with patterned waistcoats, or, even more continental, a polo-neck jumper.

▲ A variation of the chunky knit sweater and cravat, 1954.

# Everyday Dress

In Britain, men's clothing shops, which had begun the decade importing American clothes, started stocking Italian fashions, and London's Soho area became a Mecca for the stylish male in search of the latest Italian designs.

For most men the traditional sober lounge suit continued to be the normal mode of dress, often worn with a jumper or cardigan on less formal occasions, with perhaps a little sportiness introduced in the form of a bright or checked waistcoat. The American '40s fashion for wide, loudly patterned ties provided another chance to add a little raciness to an otherwise staid look.

**Men Only**, June 1952, advised its readers on building up a basic wardrobe: *'This situation occurs often enough with the young man just out of military service, who steps back into civilian life only to discover with something of a shock that his former clothes don't fit him any more.'*

*'What should the first one be? Sports jacket and trousers? . . . My own starting-point in wardrobe building would be a single-breasted two-piece informal suit – probably in a clean-surfaced fine tweed of medium tone. It would be a bit casual looking for general wear, but at least it would be a suit: and for*

▲ The sports pullover, a hand-knitted polo-neck, 1954.

*off-duty occasions it would, of course, be just as good as the sports-jacket uniform.*

*'Early on, I should add a pair of sports trousers, to be worn with the jacket of the two-piece suit to provide an alternative outfit.*

*'However, another suit would by then have become an early priority, and it could well be a complete contrast to the other, leaning strongly to smart formality. A double-breasted dark grey pinhead worsted, or a deep blue-grey with a faint fancy stripe, for example.*

*'If their owner wants to go to a dance, he goes in a lounge suit or in a hired dress-suit; not ideal, of course, but not so unreasonable as to give highest priority to the idea of having a dinner-suit of his own.*

*'So far, this is getting along towards being a useful, well-balanced "minimum wardrobe". With most men, however, the town lounge suit would be getting far too much strain, and another should be added at the next opportunity. In my judgement it might well be a less severe type than the other; it must, of course, be strictly a town-wear type, because that's where the collection most needs building up, but it could be quite a bit lighter in shade, and might also carry a bit more colour and pattern. I visualise perhaps a medium-to-light grey or blue-grey with a fancy distinctive stripe design – the kind of suit which would look well worn with brown shoes, but which would not look out of place with black footwear as an alternative. Single-breasted, I should think, but this isn't essential.'*

The single-breasted suit was recommended for those who were short and stout, preferably cut with a slim, long lapel. However, more important than the suit style were the colour and material; a smooth-surfaced material in darker tones, grey or blue, preferably with a slight stripe effect rather than plain. Some tailors advised that the jacket should be made very slightly shorter, to give the effect of a longer leg, *'which adds apparent height and therefore suggests a slimmer line'*.

By 1955 a peculiar jacket called the 'Relax jacket' or 'house jacket' began to

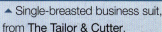

▲ Single-breasted business suit, from **The Tailor & Cutter**.
▼ Pattern for a business suit, from **The Tailor & Cutter**. The double-breasted jacket is once again cut along new, loose and long lines, with a winged collar.

appear, which, like the woman's housecoat, was designed to be worn about the house: *'They earn their keep, if only by reducing the wear and tear on your lounge suits.'* Best described as a jacket-length dressing-gown, it was a variation on the old smoking jacket, and became synonymous with the smooth, Leslie Phillips-type lady-killer.

The sports jacket, usually in tweed, was often worn for casual dress, although, as the fifties wore on, chunky sweaters became an increasing alternative. By July 1958 a reader of **Men Only** was asking: *'I have been wearing a heavy-knit sweater for casual outerwear and I have heard that knitted sports jackets are now being made which have a more finished appearance, plus, of course, the advantage of pockets. Is this much different from, say, a heavy cardigan?'* The reply was: *'Entirely different, if it's what I imagine you have heard about, namely, a normal type of sports jacket, fully tailored but cut from material which is actually knitted rather than woven. The general effect is as of a fine tweed.'* There was also the 'sweater jacket' a knitted jacket that was a kind of sports coat cum sweater.

With a sports jacket would be worn sports trousers, usually in worsted, although corduroy was, for many, an acceptable alternative. Another reader of **Men Only** wrote: *'The idea has always appealed to me to try a pair of corduroy sports trousers, mainly because they have a reputation for being particularly comfortable, as well as hardwearing. I admit they are not especially smart, but if there are no other snags I would rely on my other sports trousers for smarter occasions and get corduroy for times when a more relaxed dress could be worn.'* By 1958, *'another reasonably safe prediction this summer is a return to cord trousers. Not the corduroy of the old, thick, navy-style trouser, but thin cotton cord, strong and resilient, in a variety of colours. The trousers are cut narrow and with slanted pockets.'*

Trousers generally became narrower, following the Italian style: *'Twenty inches is considered rather wide for trouser bottoms nowadays,'* **Men Only**, November 1955. Button flies, almost universal a decade before, were now becoming old-fashioned as zips improved: *'"Sartorial Security" – A Swift exclusive self-locking zip-fastener ensures complete masculine*

peace-of-mind, since its self-springing lock safeguards against accidental opening.', advert from November 1955. Braces too became out of date, as the fashion for shirt and tie, worn without waistcoat or jumper, spread.

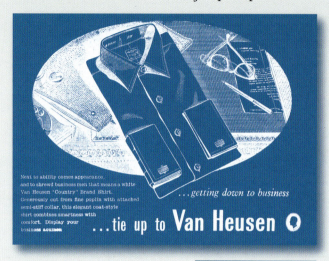

Next to ability comes appearance, and to shrewd business men that means a white Van Heusen 'Country' Brand Shirt. Generously cut from fine poplin with attached semi-stiff collar, this elegant coat-style shirt combines smartness with comfort. Display your business acumen

...getting down to business

...tie up to **Van Heusen** O

## Shirts

At the beginning of the decade, most men's shirts were still sold with removable collars, usually two: *'Radiac striped tunic shirt with two comfortable Trubenised collars'*, advert from April 1952. In November that year **Men**

▲ Shirt with attached collar, 1955. The collar stud was virtually a thing of the past by now, except on formal occasions.

▼ The style had become less formal, like this typical outfit from 1958 – chunky crew-neck sweater and cravat with open-necked shirt.

▼ The sporting look: check tweed jacket, cheese-cutter cap and brogues.

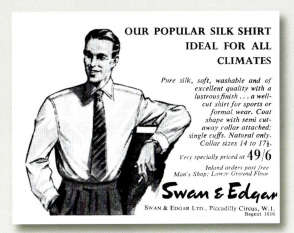

OUR POPULAR SILK SHIRT
IDEAL FOR ALL
CLIMATES

*Pure silk, soft, washable and of
excellent quality with a
lustrous finish . . . a well-
cut shirt for sports or
formal wear. Coat
shape with semi cut-
away collar attached;
single cuffs. Natural only.
Collar sizes 14 to 17½.*

*Very specially priced at* 49/6

*Inland orders post free
Man's Shop: Lower Ground Floor*

Swan & Edgar

SWAN & EDGAR LTD., Piccadilly Circus, W.1.
Regent 1616

**Only** recommended: *'A product which is very
welcome back in the shops after being absent all
through the long "Utility era" is a shirt which offers
the kind of quality associated with the "good old
days". The bodycloth is a close-woven poplin, fine but
strong. The collars and cuffs are a double-texture
fabric which is naturally semi-stiff and which gives a
smartly comfortable finish and a longer life to the
garment. An intelligent feature is that the shirt doesn't
automatically have to be bought with a regulation
"two collars". If, for example, you normally wear
white starched collars, you needn't pay for shirt-
matching collars which you would not need. If, on the
other hand, you feel you'd like more than two matching collars per shirt, there the extra collars are, ready
in stock. To make the shirt last longer still, extra cuffs
are available. The shirt costs 29s. 6d., plus collars at
2s. 9d. each. Shirts in the collar-attached style are 28s.
6d. Spare cuffs are 5s. a pair.'* This was fine if
you wanted long wear, but shirt studs were
notoriously fiddly items and the durability of
synthetic fibres and increased spending
power tipped the balance towards attached
collars, especially soft
collars. **Men Only**,
June 1952, suggested
that one invest in *'half
a dozen plain cream or
white collar-attached
shirts, suitable alike for
town or leisure wear, plus
a fine-check flannel sports
shirt and a shirt which
could be worn with a white
stiff collar.'*

By 1955 Van Heusen were advertising
their *'business shirt – coat-style shirt generously cut
from fine white poplin with an attached semi-stiff
collar'*, while detachable cuffs became a thing
of the past, as even formal shirts now sported
soft cuffs.

For leisure time, the tie-less shirt, with its
collar worn outside the jacket, continued to
be the predominant fashion. There was also
an increase in the wearing of sports shirts of
the Fred Perry type as well as the introduction
of the American bowling shirt, like a sports
shirt, but looser in the body and cut square
across the shoulders with short sleeves. By
1958, fashionable sports shirts were in
brushed cotton, as **Men Only** reported:
*'And by brushed cotton I mean what they used to call
flannelette – a very much improved version of it, by
the way – in big pastel-shaded checks. They are cheap,
cheerful, mild to the sunburned skin, and available
for wearing inside or outside the trousers, though I
gather that outside the trousers is going out of style
somewhat.'* However, *'Do not think, by the way,
that flannelette checks have it all their own way this
summer. Horizontally-striped shirts in drip-dry cotton
are also going to be popular, as are Terry-towel
shirts.'*

◄ Despite the fashion
for man-made fibres,
a silk shirt was still the
best.

◄▼ Short-sleeved,
check sports shirt,
worn open necked
(rear), standard every-
day shirt (centre) and
boy's shirt (front),
1958.

> 66
> A Swift exclusive self-locking zip-fastener ensures
> complete masculine peace-of-mind, since its self-
> springing lock safeguards against accidental opening
> 99

## Ties

The classic British tie at the start of the
decade was fairly narrow, about 3in wide at
its widest point, and short, as it was intended to be worn with a waistcoat or jumper.

Designs were fairly conservative, small repeated patterns or diagonal stripes being favourite.

Then came the American influence with wide, long ties – intended to be worn with shirt only – and loud, bright patterns. These were popular, but not in the office or among older men, where the traditional style persisted. **Men Only**, June 1952, rec-

ommended: *'Rich, deep, solid colours such as maroon, bottle-green or royal blue, are at their best when used in small areas by way of sharp contrast. Socks and ties are the obvious examples – ties particularly, because the contrast between the tie and the shirt colour is bound to be sharper and more dramatic than the contrast between socks and suit. This is particularly true when the shirt is unpatterned: a plain white or cream, say, or a pastel such as biscuit, pale grey or pale blue. Against such shirts a solid-colour tie has a clean crispness of contrast which is always very effective.'*

With the fashion for Italian suits came narrower ties, no longer just in cotton; as the following advertisement from 1955 confirms: *'There's the stamp of unmistakable quality in a tie made entirely of silk-soft suede leather, dyed in subtle plain colours including browns, blues, greens, and many other shades. Long-lasting, resilient for good knotting, and in superb taste, these ties cost 27s. 6d.',* or *'If you have always longed to own a tartan necktie, you can have your ambition gratified for a mere 9s. 6d., for which you can choose from a wide range of authentic clan tartans, in all-wool materials made in Scotland.'*

## Overcoats

Men's overcoats changed little in style. They were, after all, made for comfort rather than fashion at a time when cars were draughty and with inefficient heaters, and many people did not have a car and relied on even draughtier public transport. **Men Only**, November 1952, reported that: *'the experts reckon that the best-selling coat of 1952 – and presumably 1953 and 1954 also, because these trends don't change suddenly – will be a single-breasted style, very straight-hanging and vertical-looking, with clean-fitting, natural shoulders. Those are the classic essentials of the style, and within them there's scope for various alternative details. Side-pockets, for example. The usual kind would be patch-pockets, with a flap, but some men prefer the vertical slash opening, and it makes little difference.*

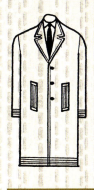

Again, the back of the coat may either have a neat half-belt or be left quite plain.

'Naturally, the character of the cloth goes with the style of the coat. Since the aim is a sleek, easy-draping straight-up-and-down effect, the material mustn't be one of those thick fleeces, such as would be right for a belted town Ulster. Instead, you need a supple tweed or Cheviot, which will drape cleanly. As a result, you get a clear-patterned cloth instead of a muzzy plain one, and the colourings prevail among the medium greys rather than among the dark greys, grey-greens, and blue-blacks.

'So, what with colour, material, and the more precise line, you see what I mean when I say that style is much less casual-looking than over-coats have been for some years past. I may add that although this single-breasted "box" coat – as the tailors call it – is as smart as they come, it also happens to be among the most comfortable. The cut is easy and unrestricted, and that clean-fitting shoulder-line seems to make the coat feel almost weightless, while leaving the warmth.

'This is a trend, not a revolution. Last year's favourite, the snug, all-round-belted, double-breasted town Ulster, with deep collar and wide lapels, is still the runner-up rather than an also-ran.'

By the mid-1950s, a straight-hanging Cheviot, single breasted, in a medium mixture colouring, or a medium to dark grey, was the general fashion, being as it was, good for general town wear and capable of being worn over both informal clothes or a dinner suit. This, alongside a lined raincoat for country wear and bad weather in town, was all a man might need in the way of coats. The water-proof virtues and lightness of synthetic mixtures, primarily cotton and nylon, were increasingly being used for both as recorded by **Men Only** in December 1955: 'Last year I bought a plastic raincoat with a Terylene reinforcement inside the plastic. It packs as small as plastic, but is more durable. That's why this year I shall have to forgo a very clever coat I've just seen which is cotton gabardine on one side and checked tweed on the other, completely reversible and at a very attractive price.'

There were alternatives: 'Point-to-point fans and chaps who like to stuff themselves into rather small sports cars, still favour the covert type of garment with the strong rows of stitching at cuffs and hem. There is nothing whimsical about this. It is a descendant of the coat favoured by Edwardian cabbies and, believe me, they needed protection on top of a hansom, and they knew how to get it! Regarded rather as a fashion item nowadays, the rows of hem stitching are ideal protection for a coat that must necessarily get creased up a lot in getting in and out of confined spaces. Available only from the better type of retailer, these garments seem to have survived the more recent unpopularity of Edwardian styling, to become part of the better-dressed man's winter wardrobe', **Men Only**, December 1955.

For some years after 1945, raincoats tended to be of the service trench-coat variety, either kept after demob or bought as part of the huge post-war government-surplus sell-off. This was so prevalent that many manufacturers actually catered for military tastes, with heavy belted Ulster styles and Air Force blue gabardines. As men slowly got tired of looking like ex-servicemen, the Raglan proofed slip-on became the fashion. This remained the mainstay of men's raincoats through to the mid-1950s, although rainwear manufacturers began to make provision for the more specialised needs of some men, particularly sports and leisure wear.

◄ Traditional heavy overcoat, but cut straight, and belt-less, from **The Tailor & Cutter**.

◄▼ A light overcoat from **The Tailor & Cutter**, once again straight and belt-less.

▲ The Edwardian-style coat.

◄ The trench coat, 1952. Many men wore either genuine ex-service raincoats and overcoats or imitation ones.

▼ Wet weather called for the mackintosh, a trilby and gloves, in this case leather.

The 1950s Look

▲ The scooter coat.
▼ Formal wedding outfit. The groom is wearing a traditional morning suit.

Golf was one of the primary men's sports, and a man cannot play golf in a long coat; for this they produced short water-proof nylon topcoats for the all-weather sportsman. Yachtsman had for the post-war years relied on the ex-Navy duffle coat, but this too was superseded by synthetic coats, and became instead the standard wear of students and artists.

The Italian influence in men's clothing led to the 'scooter coat', specially designed for riding on the latest form of transport, being shorter and narrower at the bottom than the traditional coat.

## Formal Dress

**Men Only**, April 1952, gave advice on how to dress for a wedding: *'From the clothes point of view we need only put weddings into two main categories: formal and otherwise. Moreover, whatever applies to the bridegroom must also apply to the Best Man. Not that they dress as twins down to small details, but if one of them wears formal clothes the other must do the same; or vice versa. Incidentally, a similar principle applies if the bridegroom elects to get married in uniform; he should choose his Best Man with a uniform to match, as it were.*

'Let's consider first the formal category – a wedding where, perhaps, the bride is wearing oyster-coloured satin overlaid with seed-pearls, with a cloud of fine lace veiling and a head-dress of orange-blossom; behind her there float two, four, or more bridesmaids arrayed as, say, Dresden-china shepherdesses; and as a foil to all this finery, up in the front starboard pew the bridegroom and his henchman, the Best Man, are wearing that sober but rather dashing ensemble which we call Formal Morning Dress. All will be well so long as you remember the golden rule of formal morning dress: "If any item is optional, cut it out; and of any two alternatives, choose the simpler."

'The main item, the black tailcoat, is like most other main items of dress in that it presents the least problems. Here, it may be either one-button or two-button with either notched or peaked lapels, just as you wish. The tails of the coat should extend in length to somewhere around the bend of the knee, but a couple of inches either way would not matter.

'Trousers are easy, too, because although there is in theory a good deal of choice in the pattern of the material, in fact the only designs made nowadays are all very similar really, and all quite safe; you will doubtless be offered a tasteful grey-and-black fancy-striped cheviot, to which you can safely say yes.

'All formal trousers are, of course, finished without turn-ups. You need to adjust your braces so that when you are standing normally the trousers as seen from the back completely cover the uppers of your shoe, while leaving the solid heel visible. In front, the trousers will then just rest on the instep, giving a slight "break" in the crease without looking either skimped or baggy.

'It is immaterial whether the waistcoat happens to be single-breasted or double-breasted – either is quite correct – but we ought to agree that the colour should be light grey. Black is funereal; white is vulgar; and colours such as fawn, tan, or lilac are most suited to cabinet ministers, lord mayors, and actors, who are liable to wear morning dress so often that they may feel in legitimate need of a smart change.

'Among most dress experts there happens to be a rather naive, diehard theory that the correct footwear for formal morning dress is a contrast-topped boot: i.e. a black boot but with the top part in grey or fawn leather, like a kind of spat effect. But take it from me, that ancient convention is hopelessly outdated by the facts. The contrast-top boot is a Dodo. Apart from the old craftsmen bootmakers of St. James's, I doubt if a hundred people in the entire footwear trade have even seen one.

'What you do wear is an ordinary black town shoe or boot, preferably of light weight, because the neater finish looks better. Black patent leather is not worn. Spats are out, too. At best they were only a kind of substitute for the effect of a contrast-top boot, and now they are not only unnecessary but would also be ostentatious.

'Socks may be either plain black or plain dark grey. There may be other alternatives, but don't bother with them.

▲ Pattern for a tail suit in a very traditional style, from **The Tailor & Cutter.**

◀▼ Formal wedding suit, 1954. It comprises morning tails, straight-cut, grey, collared waistcoat and grey tie.

▼ Wedding photograph, 1956. The groom is wearing a very up-to-date suit, with a long and loose jacket.

*The best shirt is a plain white one. A white ground with fine well-spaced stripes is permissible, and so also are various very pale pastel shades; but my advice is – stick to plain white. An ordinary town style, without starched cuffs, is usual nowadays.*

*As to collar and tie, be guided again by the rule of simplicity. Firmly discard all ideas of a wing collar and cravat. Instead, choose an everyday white stiff double collar, worn with an everyday shape of tie; and, in deference to ancient custom, let the tie be in some kind of silver-grey effect. Custom also demands that you wear a white flower in your left-hand lapel buttonhole. Also wear a white handkerchief to show in the breast pocket. Twin symbols of a blameless bachelordom.*

*The final two items of the ensemble – the gloves and the hat – may seem to some men to be a bit superfluous at a wedding, since there seems scarcely a chance to wear them. Nevertheless, you must have them. The hat is a topper; preferably black silk, though in summer a pearl-grey may be worn instead. The best gloves are ordinary yellow chamois. Once they would have been "wedding-grey suede", but that would be a bit pedantic nowadays.*

*I suppose there's no need for me to stress that most formal morning dress outfits, nowadays, are hired rather than owned.*

*Let's now recognise that any amount of men want to get married in a lounge suit (whether or not the bride wears a formal bridal outfit). Some lounge suits look better in the part than others, and the choice should be made from the medium-to-dark greys, blue-greys, and fancy blues. Worsted is the best material. Double-breasted is the better style, being a trifle more dressy-looking.*

*Accessories include black shoes, a white-ground shirt, a white stiff collar, and either a black Homburg or a snap-brim felt which "goes with" the suit shade. For custom's sake the tie may as well be largely silver-grey in effect.'*

Men's evening dress had not changed much. The dinner jacket was still worn for formal occasions, and for extra-special, white tie and tails. The upper and upper-middle classes regularly changed for dinner on special occasions, so the possession of a black dinner jacket was still a normal part of a gentleman's wardrobe, though the more fashionable man would go for the new single-breasted style. A correspondent to **Men Only** asked in December 1955: *'I wish to order a new dinner suit, and want to try a single-breasted model. With my double-breasted style, now outgrown, I haven't needed a waistcoat, and I'd like still to do without one with the single-breasted. Is it possible?'* The response was: *'I've seen quite a lot of men who wear their single-breasted dinner suits without a waistcoat. Some seem to manage well enough, but mostly there's a sort of unfinished, untidy effect. Why not settle for a silk cummerbund? They're neat and comfortable.'*

Another fashionable innovation was the artificial buttonhole carnation or, as they were still commonly known, the boutonniere. They cost 6s or 7s each, which was expensive, but in the long run they were a saving.

## Pyjamas

The nightshirt, whose use had diminished rapidly in the 1940s, was now relegated

to the very old or the very old fashioned. Pyjamas were almost universally worn, although some, especially younger men, wore pants and singlet to bed.

Like much else in men's attire, pyjamas remained fairly unchanged in design, although traditional fabrics were rivalled by the new man-mades, especially nylon, Terylene and Ardil. An ICI advertisement for the latter in December 1955 claimed: *'Pyjamas containing Ardil – they're the smoothest, softest pair I ever had – never irritate my skin. They're warm, absorbent, light-weight too, so I can wear them winter and summer with superb comfort. Ardil – soft as cashmere, smooth as silk, warm and absorbent as wool.'* Many men, however, found to their cost the slippery properties of the nylon pyjama/sheet combination, waking to find themselves on the floor.

## Holiday Wear

*'The prime need of the man on holiday is colour that is not ostentatious, combined with comfort that stops short of dowdiness'*, **Men Only**, 1958.

In 1955 an American manufacturer introduced *'pure rubber swim suits – no supporter needed'*. These were designed to flatten the wearer's stomach on the beach, but did not really catch on as they tended to displace the spare tyre rather than control it. The move to Italian design brought with it swimming trunks that were, by British standards, *'almost immodestly brief'*. At first these were in bright colours but by 1958 the trend, while still for the very brief, was to simple elasticised cotton trunks, often plain black. Over these you might wear the popular 'sun toga'. This was, despite its rather grandiose name (with, of course, Italian references), little more than a towel with a hole in it for your head to come out and some type of strap or belt around the middle to keep the whole thing from flapping about.

Jeans, originally work-wear, had become a growing part of teenage dress, and like many other teenage styles began to creep up the age range. They remained, however, firmly rooted in the leisure and holiday wear bracket, as did jean-style trousers, produced in canvas and other materials, of a similar cut and with pockets in a jeans configuration. All, of course, were worn with a Hawaiian-type shirt.

▼ A lightweight summer jacket, of the sort often seen in the 1950s.

Tailored jersey
by **Wolsey**

# Women

*'A plain tailored suit is an essential in every woman's wardrobe. A dozen outfits can be planned on this one basic garment.', the **Academy of Charm and Beauty**, 1953.*

## Women's

fashions during the 1940s had been driven by austerity. Shortages in materials and labour dictated simple lines, while rationing meant that clothes in general became practical rather than decorative. Added to this was a whole raft of legislation that set out how many or, more accurately, how few buttons, pleats, pockets, etc. could be incorporated in any garment. As with other wartime restrictions, people on the whole accepted them for the sake of the country, but after years of rationing women yearned for a release from such restrictions and, in spite of continued rationing, female clothing during the late 1940s became increasingly feminine, with the trend being for soft, curving lines accentuating both bust and hips, which harked back to the Edwardian era.

The 1950s have often been described as the 'Golden Age' of haute couture, coming as they did between the austerity '40s and the anything-goes '60s. Pre-war, Paris had been the undisputed centre of haute couture but this ceased with the German occupation in 1940; however, the city quickly regained this status after the war. Pierre Balmain was at that time generally regarded as the leading French designer, his main rivals being Christian Dior, who had introduced the New Look, and Cristóbal Balenciaga, who developed it.

The enforced absence of French fashion during the war years had been a boost for British and American domestic fashion houses, a situation built on in the post-war period. Soon London had established a reputation for good design, led principally by Hardy Amies and Norman Hartnell, the latter significantly enhancing the reputation of British couture when he was chosen by the then Princess Elizabeth to

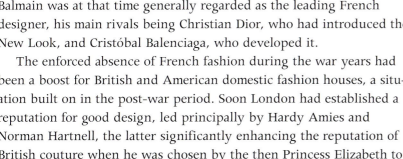

◀ The pencil dress with dolman sleeves and wide hat – the new fashion for 1951.

▲ Fashionable suits with very tight waists and pencil skirts. The suit was one of the mainstays of a woman's wardrobe.

▶ A typical 1940s outfit; note particularly the wide shoulders and headscarf.

*Marlonna* TRAVEL COATS

design her wedding dress.

Couture outfits were the result of much painstaking work, involving as they did the very best in cutting, tailoring and dressmaking skills, as well as the contribution of embroiderers, lace-makers and a host of other specialists. As such, they were, and indeed remain, prohibitively expensive for all but the very rich.

If a fashion-house dress was firmly beyond the reach of the average woman, a fashionable outfit was certainly not. For the comfortably off there had always been off-the-peg designer models: 'A fine wool dress after Pierre Balmain' ran one typical advert from Fortnum & Mason in 1954. As you might expect, being from shops such as Fortnum & Mason these dresses were towards the upper end of the couture-reproduction market, as was the price tag of 36 guineas.

Now, however, there was a new slant to the couture-reproduction market as such dresses moved down the cost ladder. The improvement in the quality of clothing worn by the average Briton during the 1930s, due to better fitting ready-to-wear garments, had continued throughout the war, though somewhat held back by rationing. Vastly upgraded methods of mass production introduced as a necessary part of the war effort were applied to clothing and other forms of peacetime manufacturing. The British and American ready-to-wear industries copied Paris high fashion with great speed and economy, and they made no pretence in the matter.

The ending of government restrictions on the supply of paper meant a rapid expansion of magazines, and through these popular

▲ Spring fashions, 1951. These include several Utility outfits as the wartime scheme was still in operation at this time.

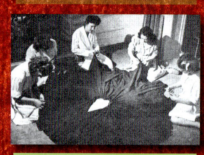

▲ Couture dresses needed vast amounts of work by skilled workers, as with this Dior dress.

▲ British couture house dress.

fashion was able to shadow haute couture developments faster than ever before. In these magazines and the newspapers experts would give advice not only on what to wear, but how to present a fashionable front on a limited income. In 1953, the **Academy of Charm and Beauty** suggested that the core of your wardrobe should be certain 'basic' clothes. What constituted basic was defined by a question: '*Can I wear it on three different types of occasions? If it's a dress – would I be equally comfortable in it at the football match, dancing, and the office?*' These basic clothes comprised a dress, a coat, two sets of accessories, (one more formal than the other), a basic suit and two sets of accessories for the suit, to be acquired in that order. The list shows just how important accessories were considered.

The following year, **Woman's Weekly** went into more detail: '*Figure is the first thing (apart from face and hair), so let's begin the first month with a really good elastic belt and brassiere. Next, invest in a petticoat and panties to match. (Nylon for preference.) In summer these will be light. For winter choose a dark colour. Nylon will make you feel like a millionairess, and it will give a smooth, non-clinging line to everything you wear over it. It can be washed in minutes and be ready to wear next morning. We'd say buy black now [July] because you are preparing for Autumn, when all your dresses will be dark. (No white petticoats under dark dresses!)*

'*Now for the coat. Choose something in a good, strong colour which will be right for any occasion, and will be interseasonal, and will look elegant with black accessories, casual with brown walking shoes. Dark green, dark red, deep blue or grey or black and white mixture will all do this.*

◀ Evening dress, 1956. Not every-one could afford such luxury.

▼ A suit, 1951. The suit was the everyday workhorse of women's dress in the 1950s.

19

CLOTHING · WOMEN

▼ Most women needed help to achieve the fashionable hourglass figure.

'*Wearing the coat, next month choose a dress. Being all in one piece will make you look slim – and taller. An all-purpose, simple wool jersey to match the coat; one with a straight skirt and high round neck and three-quarter sleeves will always be right, and with a little costume jewellery will dress up easily for after six. Lastly, with your basic outfit assured, you can indulge in a romantic black frock for dressy evenings. This might well be in black rayon taffeta.*'

The suit was universally accepted as one of the mainstays of the wardrobe. Jackets fitted very closely and there were, as such, some women who it was thought should NOT wear suits: the **Academy of Charm and Beauty** listed them: '*those who are badly over-weight, those whose buttocks measure four inches more than their bust; and women whose bust-line is four inches larger than their buttocks*'.

**Woman's Weekly**, March 1959, described the ideal suit: '*What is the ideal minimum wardrobe for a working girl? We shall certainly need a suit; one which will not be rough and tweedy. (This one can go away to wait for the rougher days of next autumn.) We shall need a smooth wool, gabardine or grey flannel. This is the outfit which will carry us into the first mild days wearing perhaps a Paisley wool blouse beneath or a jersey. In warmer weather the suit will be ideal for work or play worn with a silk or cotton top. It will form the basis of a holiday and travel outfit, and will be quite formal enough for almost all occasions according to the way we wear it.*

'*Choose shoes, bag and gloves to*

*go with this important suit, and then arrange all the rest of the items around these accessories. For instance, if you get grey accessories, let grey occur in your cotton frocks too; if navy, pond green or red, keep this colour well in mind when choosing, so that the same set can, if needed, serve with everything.*

'*Next important item is a cotton or silk suit, and this can also be worn with the same accessories. Be careful when planning this suit for later to find a material which will give practical service, and not too pale a colour if you intend to wear it out in one season. A garment is only a big success if you can live in it.*'

Next came the dress. The full-skirted, tight-waisted dress had started the whole New

▲ Several classic items make up this outfit – the pencil skirt, the short, 'bum-freezer' jacket, the low-fronted shoes, the long gloves and the cap.

▶ Accessories were all-important to an outfit.

▼ Classic wide-skirted dresses from the 1950s.

Look, and would continue to be fashionable throughout much of the decade. Not only the cut had changed but the small repeating patterns that had been such an integral part of Utility textiles were replaced by large, bold and brightly coloured patterns, often with a floral motif.

**Woman's Weekly** advised: *'Cotton frocks? Give yourself the thrill of choosing some pretty new fabrics and patterns – and we'll help you there. If what you have left over from last year are all in light colours or white, vary the choice at your disposal by adding darker colours, or prints incorporating plenty of darks.'* However: *'A gay cotton print is glamorous and heartening, but not in a large town on a dull-skied day, and crumpled after sitting for hours in an office. A mid-tone uncrushable dupion, or colour printed with a design in black would be right for warm and dull days, too, while the cotton print can be reserved for heat-waves and holidays.'*

The casual trend in clothes meant that separates became as popular as dresses. The skirt was, according to **Woman's Weekly**: *'the most useful inhabitant of your between-season wardrobe, and goes on all the year round, being becoming for innumerable occasions. Teamed rightly,*

*it can be perfect for everyday working in an office; it is positively the only sensible outfit to take away at week-ends. It goes with you on your holiday and becomes a cool-weather or hot-weather companion all the year round. So no wonder we consider that it is worthy of our most careful thought and consideration.*

*'This season [1954] the skirt is to be more serviceable and more becoming than ever. The most popular shape is slightly flared; not so full as to be big-making, and not so tight as to become seated. The material which is newest and gayest, while at the same time being utterly wearable – is plaid. It has the right weave, weight, and colour, and a light, large over-check goes over a smaller shadow check in the most charming designs. The colours are bold yet subtle, and lovely deep wool mixtures include pansy and wild orchid. Some of these plaid skirts have huge patch pockets, and many have interesting cummerbund effects at the waist. It is immensely fashionable for skirts to be worn over the top of the jersey, so the waistline itself is more than ever important. The cardigan is then slung loosely over the shoulders, buttoned at the top button only, or left open and the sleeves rucked up. Several rows of pearls, a gilt charm necklet against a black jumper, and a brilliant green and blue silk ribbon scarf tied closely and high at the neck on a brilliant blue jumper were some of the casual-looking effects we recently admired.'*

Plaid would continue to be a most popular pattern throughout most of the 1950s, used most often for sports or casual clothes – skirts, trousers and head-scarves. It was particularly popular for use in children's clothes, although it would also

regularly be used for women's skirts and trousers. In August 1952, **Woman's Weekly** advised its readers: *'Do not be afraid of the large overchecks; they will not make you look big as the under-pattern is small. They are gay and charming. (Keep in mind your overcoat scheme so that it will form part of the team.) Your twin-set can then pick out either the darkest of the colours in the skirt or the lightest.*

*Incomparably yours* fully-fashioned knitwear by **Lyle and Scott** OF HAWICK SCOTLAND

*'It is certainly a good plan, however many woollies you may own, to have at least one dark set. The new fashion of pushed-up sleeves saves some of the soiling of the light colours, but even so, pale tones are a responsibility in town or for work. They are best saved for leisure and for the country.'*

Blouses remained ever-popular, with brief sleeves or long sleeves on mannish poplin shirts that teamed with jeans. *'For slim, boyish types there are linen shirts to be worn loose with shorts, slacks or swimsuit, or tucked into a skirt'*, **Everywoman**, June 1955.

Tight sweaters became popular in the late 1940s and created 'the sweater girl' look, the main point of which was to emphasise a thrusting, conical-shaped bosom, achieved by concentric circular stitching on the brassiere. This would remain popular through to the mid-1950s. A quite different

◀ Chunky knit jumper and pleated skirt, in popular tartan, 1953. These items were seen throughout the decade.
◀ Flared skirt and twin-set, 1956. This was a standard outfit, popular for any less-formal occasion.
▼ The post-war 'sweater girl' look, 1950. This effect was achieved by the use of a specially designed bra (p.104).

A sporty leisure-wear jumper. Note the popular turned-up collar.

variation on the sweater was originally an American idea – elegant evening sweaters covered with embroidery, beads and sequins. These became popular throughout Europe as well as the USA. **Woman's Weekly**, March 1952, commented: *'It makes a very new look, and goes with the full, fabulous new skirts.'*

Jumpers, cardigans and twin-sets went very well as part of the gradual but unceasing move towards a more casual, leisure-oriented style in everyday dress, and the use of new man-made fibres meant they kept their shape better, were easier to wash and cost less.

1940s, remained, but with one great change. Where they had been loose they now became close fitting and tapered. Lengths varied from just below the knee, known as 'pirate pants', to calf length or ankle length. Then there were 'pedal-pushers' – as with so many other day-to-day fashions, these started with the new teenage market, but their use spread rapidly up the age range, representing as they did a young look.

The pinny remained the housewives' main work robe. The old tunic-style pinny continued to be the uniform of older women, while their younger sisters dressed in something a little less severe. The latter donned a

> A friend of mine says that film stars do not wear any undies beneath these sheath dresses, and that is the reason they cling like a second skin.

The sweater and the cardigan virtually became symbols of the 1950s. Tight jumpers or cardigans, which showed the hour-glass shape so important in the early 1950s, were worn by women of all ages, either individually or as twin-sets, while the evening sweater became very popular. Later, as styles and body shapes relaxed, chunky-knit sweaters were favoured, with a cashmere jumper or hat an expensive variation.

Trousers, which had become so much a part of women's clothes in the

waitress-style apron, tied at the back, usually with a bib, but the whole often 'glamorised' with frilly edging or Tyrolean-style embroidery. The housecoat was worn for more heavy duty housework. This came either in the form of a full-length overall, front buttoning or zippered rather like a dressing gown, but tight-waisted, following the fashionable dress style, or as a half-length, full affair rather like a maternity smock. Both styles were often fitted with large patch pockets for practicality.

Beaded sweaters, an American idea, became very fashionable for evening wear.

The raincoat made a comeback as a fashion garment, tightly belted, but with its belt tied rather than clasped, it had a sophisticated, continental air. At the other end of the scale a fur coat summed up the desire for luxury after the drab years of austerity. Fur became a status symbol that stayed fashionable throughout the 1950s, often used as trimming to collars and cuffs and even on negligées. Mink was the most desired, and upper-class magazines such as **Vogue** carried many adverts for it: *'stoles – many luxurious designs with detachable tails. Ranch mink from 125 gns., silver blue from 195 gns., sapphire from 350 gns., including purchase tax'* [July 1955]. For those who could not afford to buy a new coat when their old one became unfashionable there was an alternative: *'Coats restyled to model*

◀ A classic outfit, 1954. The tight-waisted, chunky knit jumper and the equally figure-hugging slacks in tartan mean this could only be the 1950s.

▲ The sweater remained popular throughout the decade.

◀ The classic 1950s housewife wearing the classic housewife's uniform, the pinny, 1952.

*jacket for only 10 gns.'* (July 1955). Shops also offered a trade-in on your old model. Other popular luxury furs included leopard and ocelot, but for the masses who could not afford a real mink coat, fake fur was a very acceptable alternative. An example of this was 'Furleen', by Astraka, whose top-of-the-range 'Minkaleen' jacket cost 20 guineas in 1953, which was still a lot of money but far cheaper than the real thing. Most women had at least one fur coat, either an expensive fur, or a cheaper version such as rabbit or fake fur. These were not only a luxury but in an age where most houses and cars were draughty, they could be a necessity on a cold winter's night.

With increased leisure time and more money to spend, women in the 1950s experimented with different evening styles. For formal occasions women still wore floor-length ball gowns, but varying from the wide-skirted, tight-waisted New Look to the body-hugging sheath dress. Shiny satins were sprinkled with sequins and rhinestones and attention focused on the bust. With strapless gowns in particular, support for the figure was essential, and many dresses came complete with integral boning and stiff petticoats. One correspondent to **London Life** magazine in May 1954, asked: *'Though I have a good figure and like clothes, and long to wear one of those slinky close-fitting evening dresses that look as if one has been poured into a silver sheath, I never manage to look anything but a lump in them. A friend of mine says that film stars do not wear any undies beneath these dresses, and that is the reason they cling like a second skin. Is that true?'* The response was that: *'Only the briefest of undies could be worn, and some years ago these metallic sheath dresses were coated with an adhesive stuff inside. The star wriggled into them, the adhesive stuck and clung – and there was the effect you seek.'*

Shorter length cocktail dresses also came into fashion and Chanel produced more relaxed evening styles. The flying panel, which as its name suggests was a loose panel, rather like a cape, became a popular

► Make Mine Mink, 1955. Whether it was a jacket, a stole or a full coat, ocelot, mink, rabbit or even fake, every woman simply had to have a fur.
► A very striking piece of underwear.
► ► Cartoon from the **Blighty** annual showing the two main dress fashions of the period: the straight dress and the flared. Note also the classic 1950s figure shapes.

feature on both long and short evening dresses.

Wedding dresses followed the fashionable line, becoming tight waisted. For the first half of the decade the fashion in wedding dresses was full length, with long sleeves, usually full at the top and tight from the elbow, often with medieval-style shaped cuffs. The main variations were in collar shape, which tended to follow the fashion for evening dresses – V-necked, high- necked, bateau-necked and scalloped among other styles. A common theme was a long veil, often with a floral headpiece, sometimes over a pill-box hat, once again looking very medieval. Brides in the later 1950s often wore far plainer dresses, with short sleeves, or even sleeveless. The veil was still there, but minus the floral headpiece, and the neckline, following the fashion for evening dresses, was wide and curved.

Pregnancy had never quite shaken off the Victorian image of a necessary evil, during which women should stay firmly out of sight. When it was absolutely necessary to emerge into the public view, smocks and wrap-around skirts were the answer.

However, the end of the war and the return of so many husbands and boyfriends led first to a rash of marriages, then to a baby boom, and pregnancy began to be viewed in a different light. Maternity wear became something to be proud of, and dresses, suits, evening wear and even beachwear for expectant mothers were widely available.

Nightdresses with matching negligées were very much a feature of the period, fashionably made from nylon or another man-made fibre, such as 'Celshung' (an acetate fabric), and were usually fairly long with frills around the neck and hem. Later the fashion was for shortie nightdresses, also known as baby-doll nightdresses, which flared from the neck to a hemline just past the bottom, usually worn with matching panties. As a contrast to this feminine laciness, a man's dressing gown, or a more expensive woman's version, cleverly cut to look like a man's dressing gown, might be also worn, usually of the long, silk variety.

The fashion for wide skirts meant that glimpses of women's underwear were more common than ever before. Circular skirts,

◄ ▲ Top-of-the-range wedding dress, 1954.
▲ The pencil skirt might not seem an ideal fashion for maternity wear, but no, Gor-ray had the answer, 1958.
◄◄◄ Maternity dress, March 1951. Pregnancy ceased to be something to hide and maternity outfits were fashionably designed.
◄◄ The 'shortie' nightdress; you can just see the matching pants.
◄ Pyjamas, 1955.

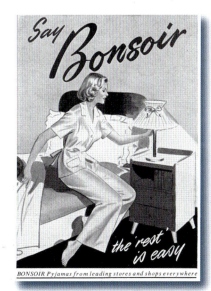

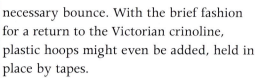

necessary bounce. With the brief fashion for a return to the Victorian crinoline, plastic hoops might even be added, held in place by tapes.

**Woman's Weekly**, August 1951, advised its readers that: *'Petticoats matter in summer. People sit about more on the grass, in deck chairs, and the wind easily blows a light skirt about. What you wear beneath becomes as important as your dress and must be as freshly laundered. A light coloured slip is right beneath a light printed dress, but, it is much better to wear a dark petticoat under navy or black. Especially is this important if the skirt has a slit. It is far from entrancing, as the man said, to see white frills, or off-white lace and off-pink scallops suddenly appearing to arrest the eye in the wrong place! Next time you invest in a nylon slip, think in terms of dark as well as your light dresses, and remember that winter is only around the corner.*

*'Perhaps you feel that it is unnecessary to wear a slip under a wool frock, but the advantages of doing so are several. Any skirt hangs more smoothly with a neat sheath of some silky material beneath. The back of the skirt will not "seat" so readily, especially if the underslip is cut on the straight. Also the warmth of the complete envelope of silk is comforting.*

*'Maybe you have an elderly black satin evening skirt you can cut up when you have time for a little sewing job? Anyway, let's take the male hint and snap out of "white only" and pink-mindedness about petticoats!'*

designed to flare out while dancing, and short tennis skirts added to this.

Big pants, of the games knickers variety, were the answer. On the other hand, tight dresses, such as the sheath, created another problem that would now be called 'visible panty line'. With these dresses pants were often either worn under the girdle or even omitted altogether.

The latest man-made textiles were perfect for underwear, as **Woman's Weekly**, August 1958, pointed out: *'Drip-dry materials, underwear and stockings take only a few minutes to launder. There is no excuse for lack of freshness.'*

In many ways the most important piece of 1950s female underwear was the petticoat. Balmain designed a range of dresses for younger women with full underskirts of stiffened net, topped with lace or tulle. To present a successful New Look, or A-line, lace or net petticoats had to be fluffed out by layers of stiffened muslin, ruffled taffeta or sugar-washed nylon frills to give the skirt its

The item of swimwear most famous at this time was the bikini, first called the bikini suit. **London Life**, April 1955, declared: *'Bikinis are all the rage, even tartans and stars.'* However, most women still wore a one-piece swimming costume, with a skirted look, either short and clinging or longer and flared. The reason was of course that many women did not have the figure for a bikini, and others did not have the nerve to wear what their mothers would find shocking. For those without the figure, the one-piece could contain a boned top and cross-over

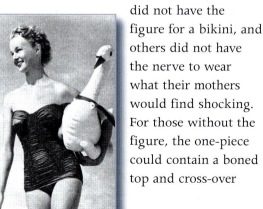

A candlewick dressing gown in a men's style became the height of fashion, as seen here in **Vogue**, July 1955.

A range of nightwear in nylon, including the very fashionable 'shortie' pyjamas and nightdress, 1959.

A classic swimsuit which could have come straight from the 1920s.

Bikini, mid-1950s. A very typical ruched bikini of the period; note the large pants, which would not become brief until the later years of the decade.

A wet-look, ruched swimming costume, 1954. Growing wealth and higher wages meant that holidays and therefore leisure wear became increasingly important.

support for the stomach, on similar lines to a girdle. By the later 1950s the popular style of one-piece had a shirred body often in a wet-look material, with or without a skirt, all worn, of course, with a rubber swimming cap often covered with rubber flowers or large rubber petals, so that the whole thing became a flower.

# Fashions Year by Year – 1950

At the fashion shows the New Look was superseded by the 'body line', a shapely silhouette with an emphasised but unexaggerated bust, an angular hipline, long legs and a natural shoulder line. All of this was epitomised by the 'sheath' dress, with its pencil-slim skirt, shorter than the previous year's fashion. The sheath had a small waist and tight skirt and was worn unbelted, the wearer squeezing herself into the required shape with a suitably severe foundation. Dior called his the 'vertical' line.

The sheath was also the most fashionable evening line, although some afternoon and evening ensembles retained wide skirts that made a feature of wide collars and a tiny waist. One alternative was a balloon-shaped gown.

Suits had skirts that continued the straight, narrow cut of dresses, while the jackets were often close fitting and low buttoned, with horseshoe collars. A streamlined 'middy' blouse was worn to go with the 'vertical' line.

Everything had to be co-ordinated: blouses matched the suit or its collar; dresses matched top coats or their linings. White teamed with a contrasting dark colour was much in evidence, and much emphasis was placed on accessories. Fabrics for both day and evening wear were luxurious: chiffon, net, tulle, organdie and muslin, while taffeta was often used for dresses and coats.

Coats could either be hip or full length, while the collars were small or non-existent; alternatively there were shawl collars and double-breasted coats. A particular novelty was the 'trumpet' coat, straight from the hips, then flaring from the knee.

The high-street version of the sheath frock was adapted for the vast majority with less than perfect figures, who, unlike their couture-wearing sisters, could not afford the expensive foundation garments that could cover this up. It incorporated a belt that would be pulled tight to accentuate the waist. Like their couture originals, they often sported a large collar.

## 1951

There was little change from the lines of the preceding year. Halter necks reappeared, and the 'trumpet skirt' followed the trumpet coat. Jackets were either fitted or had a 'swing-back' shape. Popular colours were grey, black, navy and neutral. Dior and Balenciaga displayed a heavy Chinese influence, using mandarin collars, straight edge-to-edge jackets and coolie hats.

In London debutante-style tiered ball gowns and evening dresses were much in evidence. The most common styles in top coats were a formal, fitted, high-waisted princess silhouette and the tent line.

For the ordinary woman, American raincoats were popular, being both flattering and practical, as fabric-proofing was advanced and manufacturers employed

Parisian couturiers to design them. From the USA too came the smock top, which could be worn with trousers or with a flared or straight skirt, and denim jeans began their inexorable march into the fashion market.

**Everywoman**, March 1951, advised its readers: *'Suits are streamlined, classic, with womanly hiplines; many have their own waistcoat fronts. Coats display new sleeve interest in triple puffs, deep-folded shoulder seams, unusual cuffs. The three-quarter topper is cut straight in a smooth cloth or belted in a velour tweed. Pleated skirts remain. Slim skirts are varied at times by a flare from the knees [the trumpet line]. Navy-blue, caramel and grey are first-choice colours; tailored buttons and white edgings favourite trimmings.'*

*Tailored jersey by Wolsey*

**Woman's Weekly** that January gave advice on accessories for a coat: *'in the new bottle-green shade'*, in line with the emphasis on accessories: *'Your coat will look very smart, teamed with a black velvet hat, a black patent leather handbag and patent leather shoes. Your gloves can be black suede or black kid. If you can obtain large jet buttons for your coat, this would be a very up-to-date finishing touch.'*

ALWAYS AT THE TOP OF THE FORM —

**KG** Regd.
**BRASSIÈRES**

*A wide variety of Utility and Lux tested Non-Utility Brassières, Suspender belts and Girdles, Obtainable from all good-class stores.*

Style 104 in Peach, White, Blue and Heavydew Nylon of Cambric. Sizes 32x36. As illustrated.

HOWARD WALL LIMITED, 27 HACKNEY RD., LONDON, E.2

dresses · ensembles

▲ Everyday clothes by haute-couture designers. The humble raincoat became a fashion statement, with hood and tight belt to show off the fashionably small waist.
▲◀ The 'Jennifer suit', a variation on the sports trouser suit, for leisure wear.
◀ A collection of suits and dresses, Utility and non-Utility, showing the range of fashionable shapes and cuts.

▲▲ The pencil dress with dolman sleeves and wide hat - the new fashion for 1951.
▲ Advert for Utility (hard wearing and purchase-tax free) and non-Utility (frills and fripperies) underwear, 1952. Non-Utility, of course, won, and Utility was soon to disappear.

## 1952

The London haute couture collections focused on texture rather than colour, concentrating on grey and beige, whereas in Paris colour was extensively used, especially reds, pinks, oranges and greens. There was a choice of silhouette: straight and square, soft and round, or puffed, curved and extravagant. Suit jackets tended to have set-in sleeves, cut-away fronts and extra-wide revers which extended down to a low waist fastening. Alternatively, there were straight, belted Norfolk jackets or box jackets. Skirts were generally triangular, cinched lightly at the waist and flaring. Pleated skirts remained the fashion, either alone or worn as part of a suit. They tended to be longer than previously was the case, about 12in from the ground.

Dresses had bodices that rolled softly over the bosom and then hugged the ribs. The little black dress was recommended town wear for any occasion. It could be either fitted, double-breasted or have a halter or deep V-neck.

Women's magazines described the latest haute couture trends to their readers, most of whom could never aspire to own such garments but could sport a good imitation, either through a clever choice of off-the-peg garments or through good needlework, done by a dressmaker or by themselves. *'Many of the prettiest summer frocks this year are on such simple lines that they call for a touch of trimming to add charm and the "good" look of the frock'*, **Woman's Weekly** wrote in April, reviewing that spring's shows. The concept of that season's colour was a boon to the less well-off, but fashion-conscious woman and **Woman's Weekly** continued: *'With a grey tweed suit, a green-and-white striped satin scarf looked good folded into the neck, and with it was worn a green hat to match.*

*'A slim grey flannel dress with three-quarter sleeves, shown with a straw boater hat in deep pink straw. It had a plain band of wide grey petersham ribbon round the crown, and two generous deep pink carnations exactly matching the hat were pinned on one shoulder.*

*'Another suit had a bright tan belt, buttons in the same sort of leather, as well as shoes to match, and a spry, small tan feather at the side of a grey hat. Yet another grey flannel suit was set off by sand gloves and a matching sand-coloured homburg hat. The yellow and grey scheme appeared all the time in many variations.'*

International travel was a luxury in post-war Britain and for the vast majority holidays were confined to British seaside resorts or the countryside, and for many a trip to the big cities, especially London, was a particular treat. **Woman's Weekly** that July advised its readers who might be planning such a trip that: *'The clothes you will wear about the streets will serve you best in every way if they are made of*

Evening outfit: strapless top, stole, pencil skirt and multi-string pearls around neck and wrist.
Short, waisted cardigan, worn over a dress, 1953.
Knitted waistcoat, suitable daywear for an office worker.
Cold-weather outfit with wrap-around scarf and matching 'Jester' hood, 1953.
Advert for Aertex sports shirts; note also sunglasses and hairstyles.

uncrushable material, such as silk jersey, slub rayon, uncrushable linen, or any of the many new fabrics on the market which are specially manufactured to keep us from looking crumpled when away from our friendly iron. Also it is as well to have something fairly dark in your wardrobe for hard wear without soiling. Navy blue, grey, slate blue, or dark green are very smart in hot weather if worn with some light touch such as a hat, scarf, or belt, or posy of flowers.

'A suit or a long coat with dresses under are good alternatives for sightseeing and shopping, and the same outfit will serve for travelling, with a really comfortable pair of shoes with medium heels. It will be necessary to have at least one change of shoes, and if space permits, you might like to take one pair of court slippers with heels, and one pair of flatter shoes for excursions.

'For the summer months it will be more comfortable if gloves are either cotton fabric, nylon, or crochet mesh, and all these may be washed out in a hotel hand-basin overnight. Shoes with punched holes in them are a blessing, and a hat with a small brim is

▶ A selection of fashion sweaters, 1953.
▼ Cold-weather leisure wear for skating or walks in the country etc.

kinder in a glare than a mere cap, or toque, or bonnet shape. Short sleeves on dresses will look perfectly right as long as little gloves are worn, and seven-eighths length sleeves are cooler and smarter than full length.'

On the other hand, the same magazine had that January recommended clothes for a long weekend in the country: 'Your brown overcoat would be very nice for travelling, but leave your black accessories at home. Plain brown shoes will be better.

'Wear a skirt and a twin set under the coat and put in your most solid pair of brown shoes, with flat or low heels, and perhaps rubber soles. (It would be awkward to have to refuse to go for walks through not having suitable shoes.) Wear a gay scarf and a beret to match (or a brown hat if you have it, packing a beret and a scarf).

'Warm gloves or mittens for walking and suede ones for church and travelling, and it would be wise to invest in one pair of lisle stockings. (Getting up in the morning you can put on the skirt and twin set or other jersey and stay in that outfit all day.) The shoes you travelled in will do for changing into when you come in from walks. A tweed suit would be invaluable, and it would be as well to take a mackintosh.

'For a festive evening a ballet-length frock would be excellent. (Your hostess would have warned you ahead if there are to be any full evening occasions needing a more formal dress.) Otherwise a warm wool dress will be useful.'

# 1953

The coronation of Queen Elizabeth II that June focused worldwide attention on Britain, and her coronation robes brought acclaim to British fashion designers, who took the opportunity to create a series of court-inspired clothes and to promote traditional British fabrics. The coronation influenced the colours and lines of evening dresses – white, pink, gold, mushroom and beige, and Norman Hartnell, the designer of the coronation gown, based his entire spring collection on white and gold. English tweed was the dominant fabric for day wear, while the London autumn collections used much lace for evening wear.

The previous year's high-waisted, narrow line remained largely unchanged, although the unfitted neckline and the high-length belt were two additions. Dior introduced the 'tulip' line, with a long body rounding out over the bust and shoulders in petal-shaped curves, while his hemlines rose 4 or 5in. In Paris the 'directoire' line, with long, lean sheaths, and the Victorian crinoline were revived, with rigid integral frame and stiffened material, often taffeta.

**Woman's Own**, in October that year, reported that: *'[In London] Suits are slim, well-bred, with the minimum of trimming, leaving the superb quality of fabric and cut to catch the eye.'* Whereas: *'Dresses have a fluid line, rounded from the hips before fading out at the hem, fullness swept to the back, panelled smoothly from the ribs in the princess manner, always creating a pretty, rounded bosom.*

*'Clothes are more colourful, though, because of the greater use of red.'*

In Rome, the article continued: *'Italy's new fashions are a characteristic clash of colour and mood – stark simplicity of cut by day, contradicted by wild extravagance for after-dark; vivid colours used splashily under the sun but softened down at night with a heavy shadowing of black. The elegant white that Paris is promoting now for winter has been the* choice of elegant Italians all summer long; even for travelling. Velvet again makes a sweeping entrance for a gala evening.'

And in Paris:
*'Dior's black and white check suit shows the new full-at-the-top line. Black astrakhan borders the collar, fastening and sleeves of a coat in muted brown by Dior. More has happened in Paris than the shortening of skirts. Fur – real or shaggy – lines or trims nearly every top coat and suit, and you must carry a fur muff as well. There is a great revival of black satin.*

*'Colours keep to the black and white ruling, spiced with all the golden browns, the apricots, sherry and tobacco shades. Lighting up time brings on white, faintly washed with coffee, green, blue or pink. In contrast there are intensely brilliant blues, reds, and greens in silks and satins.'*

**Woman's Weekly** welcomed the return of the fuller dress: *'Among all the talk about slim lines, pencil shapes and streak silhouettes, we may begin to wonder about the dear, useful, and charming wide skirt in which we square danced and went to parties all last winter. Is it right out of the running and must it be discarded?*

*'This would be a mistake, for there is nothing so pretty as a wide and sweeping hemline, giving grace and movement and generosity to the evening occasions when we relax. To spend all our time as slender wisps would be dull in the extreme, so thank goodness we may once more wear our felt swirls and our satin flares with joy and confidence.'*

◄ A very stylish outfit: tight, sleeveless and collarless top worn with widely flaring dress, 1953.

▲▲ Extremely fashionable short, flaring jacket, with black pencil skirt, long gloves and silly hat. The long feather was to give height and so was to be avoided if you were tall.

▲ Shorts and a short-sleeved version of the jumper comprised beachwear in 1953.

◄◄ Wearing a belt over a waisted sweater emphasised the slim waist that fashion demanded. If you had one, you flaunted it!

◄ Waisted sports jumper, with pleated skirt, beret and, of course, gloves.

## 1954

Dior introduced the 'H' line. This suggested *'the tapering figure of a young girl'* by increasing the distance between the hips and the bust. His suit jackets, which flared gently from the waist, were narrow shouldered, flat fronted and were worn with slender skirts. On the other hand, clothes from London included set-in sleeves and square shoulders for the first time since the end of the Second World War, and navy blue and grey replaced beige as the fashionable colours.

Softness was the main theme of London's autumn collections. Dresses, for example, had tie belts rather than belts with buckles. Coats were narrow to the hem and collarless or had huge cape-like collars. Tweed remained in vogue, or towelling, often of an extremely fine weave, while fur was in prominence in both London and Paris. The preferred length for coats was two-thirds or seven-eighths.

Hubert de Givenchy rose to fame designing clothes for Audrey Hepburn in the film **Sabrina Fair**. Hepburn's short sculpted tops had 'bateau' necklines (a sort of long, sideways, slightly down-curving, slit) and cropped sleeves – with her slight figure and short, fringed hair she epitomised the fashionable ideal of the pretty urchin, the gamine. At the other extreme was Marilyn Monroe: furs, diamonds, high heels and plunging necklines were her trademarks, effectively summing up

the aspirations and the affluence of the day.

**Woman's Own**, that February, reported: *'The silhouette for spring is essentially simple. Clothes take on the smooth, unbroken line, shed the frill and the exaggerated detail. Skirts are slightly shorter. They are often bell-like from a moulded torso and waists are left unmarred by belts or seams. The detail comes in the cut of a bodice, line of a sleeve, shape of a neckline – often high, or shaped to a wide V.*

*'Emphasis goes above the waist: narrow pleating, seam detail, pockets, all serve to flatter the bustline.*

*'Shoulders are gently rounded, a theme carried on in both coats and suit jackets with great success. Coats are often narrow, whittled to slimness at the hem. The rounded shoulder line usually flows to collarless neckline, while ribbed wool or leather collars and cuffs are currently popular on suit jackets.*

*'Although the straight skirt is still fashionable, many suits have a flared skirt from a tiny, well-fitted jacket. Tweeds are still in favour, rough or smooth, they're right for smart town wear, dresses, coats or suits.'*

**Woman's Weekly**, in September, described the autumn collections: *'Many of the new dark silk "party frocks" are the same length as day dresses, with a full skirt, shaped bodice and round or scoop neck. But it is the trimming which*

▲ Housecoat, pyjamas and negligée.
▶ In 1954 pink was all the rage – note her lipstick.
▶ A fur stole, the height of elegance.
▼ A very sophisticated outfit: tight jumper with belt, chunky jewellery, gloves and a bucket bag.

*makes them special – trimming of short silk fringe, silk braid, black velvet ribbon or velvet rouleau.'*

Holiday wear remained an important area. **Woman's Weekly**, in August, recommended a blazer worn over a dress that *'will look much more dashing when a crest is added to the pocket'*. In July it suggested you: *'take only those [clothes] which will be amiable after being packed. Swim-suit, beach wrap and shoes, towel, sun-glasses and a beach bag go in the bottom of the suitcase; it would be a tragedy to forget one of these items.*

*'An attractive and dashing cotton skirt or two will prove ideal travel and holiday companions. They will make you feel gay and pretty, and they will walk out with a sun-top, a plain cotton blouse, a wool jersey or an evening, thin blouse. (Slacks and shorts will probably be your daily wear at the sea.) A twin-set or cardigan can hardly be left out, ever. It will be the insurance against cold weather, and the cardigan can be slung over the shoulders with a cotton frock in the evenings.'*

Foreign travel was slowly becoming more common, and advice on what to wear was a common topic in that summer's magazines. For very hot places, the correct underwear was vital. A brassiere and a half-length petticoat would leave the waist free and cool, while pull-on stretchable pantie-briefs could be worn with no stockings or with half-length hose for formal occasions. The cotton dresses and other frocks for wearing in high temperatures should be chosen to give the utmost airiness around the neck and arms. **Woman's Weekly** continued: *'If you wish to look especially elegant and yet be very cool, wear the sleeveless cotton frock and add short white cotton or nylon gloves.'*

## 1955

The waist was losing its prominence as most designers concentrated on long, straight, slender lines, such as Cavanagh's 'tube' dresses and suits. Dior's 'H' line evolved into the 'A' line, coats, suits and dresses that flared from narrow shoulders to wide triangles, the waist being the cross-piece of the A. This might be positioned under the bust in the Empire style or alternatively on the hips. Natural colours – grey, fawn and a new coppery-brown – were much in evidence, while popular materials included alpaca, linen, shantung and, once again, tweed.

In London the line was soft, accompanied by sashes, scarves, bows, pleats and rolled collars. The main fabrics were tweed, sheep-skin, silk and surah. Many coats were made of stiff, bright hessian and were lined with material that matched the dress or its sash.

In the Paris autumn shows the close-fitting, unbelted sheath was prevalent for both day and evening wear. The emphasis shifted to the top with stoles and cape coats to create an outline reminiscent of the 1930s, a similarity added to by hats pulled down over the brows and high collars. There was a return to the oriental look, with straight jackets and tunics and Mandarin collars.

By now the gap between what the fashion houses were producing and what ordinary women were wearing was beginning to grow once again. As the decade wore on, a more relaxed, leisure-orientated style evolved for everyday clothes. Even high-fashion maga-zines, such as **Vogue**, showed more and more illustrations of women in casual clothes.

July's **Vogue** showed a range of summer separates: short denim shorts, medium-length cotton shorts, linen Bermuda shorts, thigh-length cotton jeans, slightly tapered tailored cotton slacks and slim jersey tights (these worn like slacks, rather than instead of stockings), all worn with a variety of tops, shirts and jerseys, worn outside. There was also a suit of thigh-length jeans and match-ing shirt. In more formal surroundings dress-es were waisted and flared to mid-thigh; large floral patterns and stripes abounded. Furs; coats, jackets and stoles were common, while suits were tightly waisted with long slightly flaring skirts.

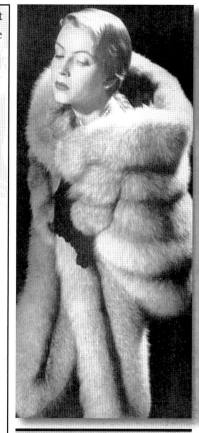

▲ Every woman's dream, every husband's nightmare.
▼ A Tyrolean-style pinafore. The pinny remained the housewife's uniform, but they were often very bright and decorated.

▶ Shocking pink –
jumper and slacks
with long, flapper-
style beads.
▶▼ Leisure wear in
the form of a knee-
length trouser suit,
1955.
▼ Nylon imitation-
fur jacket – nylon
was the new thing.
▼▼ beachwear
comprising shorts
and top, a beach
dress and even the
1950s equivalent of
a 'hoody'.

# 1956

In Paris that spring directoire-style dresses appeared once again, alongside cropped jackets at Dior and Lanvin-Castillo. In London the spring colours were again gentle and natural and there were lots of flowered prints and large hats swathed in tulle, while hips, shoulders and waistline were decorated with jewelled brooches.

By autumn black had replaced pink as the primary colour, used with grey, bronze and brown. There was an Edwardian revival at some fashion houses which included accessories such as muffs and long, flat handbags, and the use of Prince of Wales check was a seasonal favourite. Capes appeared everywhere, while in Paris many of the top coats narrowed to the hem, continuing the previous year's 'Y' line. Both capes and coats were lined with fur, which was also widely used for a range of hats - busbies and shakos, Cossack hats and even Robinson Crusoe-style cone-shaped affairs.

On the street much remained the same; summer dresses were full skirted, with plain bodices, low, round necks and

sleeveless, worn with small, flower-pot hats or large straws. Suit jackets were hip length and mostly waisted, worn with either straight or flared skirts, although some fuller, unwaisted jackets were making an appearance. Topcoats were similarly straight, but unwaisted, camel or tweed being most popular. Tweed also remained popular for suits, especially heavy, coarse tweed, often flecked, while buttons for both suits and topcoats were fashionably covered in matching material. Evening dresses were longish, either finishing at the bust with straps, often in a halter-neck arrangement, or a more full, shirt-top arrangement with short sleeves. Hats were mainly of the small, often pill-box variety.

## 1957

The fashionable line this year was simple, almost shapeless. Givenchy introduced what became known as the 'sack' dress. An advert for Pure Lemon Juice the following February pointed out that: *The "sack" leaves room for the imagination. Employing the principle of the yashmak, it enchants by hinting. In one form or another it is catching on – and there's the danger. For those of us who are plump, the 'sack' is the greatest menace since the invention of roly-poly pudding.*

*'Make no mistake. The "sack" is not a dust sheet beneath which the figure can be hidden and forgotten. On the woman who has a slender figure it performs a sinuous undulation. On the rest of us, it remains sadly a sack.'*

Dior unveiled the 'spindle', or chemise, line; slim yet loose, rather like a nightshirt, the dress was waist-less and narrowing towards the hem. Chanel once again produced cardigan-jacket suits for daywear, with the addition of soft blouses that matched the coat linings, and ankle length, bias-cut gowns for evening. One break from the loose fit was Dior's short,

FOR CLASSICS

◄ Long, straight bulky overcoats, ideal with straight skirts.
▼ Suit with asymmetric jacket and pencil skirt, bulky overcoat and, of course, gloves.
▼◄ The tweed suit, standard everyday dress throughout much of the decade.

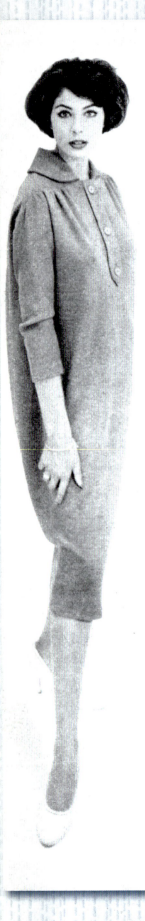

tight, Saharienne jacket, which was cinched at the waist.

Everyday fashion was becoming increasingly youth-led, as the now firmly established teenage market began to spread its effect upwards. The trend was towards colourful, amusing clothes, smart and decidedly modern, yet free enough to allow the wearer to take part in leisure activities – dancing, bowling or riding on the back of a scooter or motor bike.

## 1958

Saint Laurent introduced the wedge-shaped 'trapeze' dress, which sloped from the shoulders to a widened hem, falling just below the knees, with a simple collar, no cuffs and one bow above its high waist. Dresses and jackets were generally collarless, with narrow sleeves and no cuffs. Waistlines were high to balance the high hem. Jackets were similarly short, ending at the hipbone. Cardin resurrected the 'puff-ball' skirt.

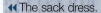

You're smart if you're seen in the **GOR-RAY** set

PRINCESS    GRANDEES    BALTIMORE

**CUDDLE**  This is a whirl of warmth. It has deep, unpressed pleats, and there's lots of cunning design behind its casual, comfortable 'chic. In the loveliest woollens, and the gayest tweeds. 52/6 to 87/6 approx.

**GRANDEES**  Perfect partner for your sweaters and blouses. Tailored to slim the hips, edge-stitched pleats at front and back swing out gaily as you walk. 59/6 to 92/6 approx. O.S. 55/- to 105/- approx. For 5'2"s 55/- to 67/6 approx.

**PRINCESS**  Inimitably tailored with a sleek hip-line and wide swing of edge-stitched pleats which always keep their shape. 47/6 to 72/6 approx.

**BALTIMORE**  A fashionable 'butterfly' kick-pleat at the back—each edge-stitched fast—for always! 35/6 to 59/6 approx. O.S. 65/- to 72/6 approx.

CUDDLE

**GOR-RAY** *skirts one better!*
with pleats as permanent as any pleats can be

◀◀ The sack dress.
◀ The puff-ball dress, an haute-couture fashion that few women copied. As the decade wore on the gap between fashion-house creations and high-street fashions widened.
◀▼ The ever faithful wrap-around apron.
▼▼ A whole range of skirt styles, from the pencil, through the pleated straight skirt to the full flared skirt. You could choose any – what was important was the narrow waist and full hips.
▼ Dresses for older women – the straight dress was now universally worn as day wear.

Dior showed a double wedge line in suits, with a simple middy top flaring slightly to the hem, matched with a flared skirt. This loose, waistless shape was happily taken up by pregnant women, and those with larger waistlines. By the autumn Saint Laurent's trapeze-line dresses and suits had become very much the fashion and were enthusiastically adopted by the young, for whom they fulfilled the double requirements of modernity and freedom, and on whom they looked good.

Coats were generally big and bulky to match the loose dresses, knee length with high waists, wide slit necks and simple set-in sleeves. A variation was the cocoon, with a large cape collar, loose top and kimono sleeves.

One of the most popular casual looks combined tight, black ski trousers with a loose mohair or jersey top and brightly coloured costume jewellery.

fancy knit

*'As a child, I explored my grandma's attic and found a collection of shoes and dresses — "sacks", and pointed, long toed monstrosities. I remember my own feelings of pity that women of that age were forced to wear such clothes, I wondered how the menfolk could put up with their wives so dressed, and was thankful I'd missed it all. For me would be the tailored, pleated skirts and round toes. Now I must watch my daughter slip back into that period I disliked.'*

## 1959

**Woman's Companion**, of November, advised its readers that: *'For years pink has been the forgotten sister on the colour chart but like all unfashionable things it comes back full blast, and now you can't go wrong with it. Choose pink for at least one of your holiday frocks, for your new straw hat to go with the navy or grey suit, for your delicate fresh chiffon scarf, for your crisp blouse or soft dance dress.'*

In May **London Life** reported that: *'Italy gives way to the craze for 1920 styles in clothes. Note the long beads, short skirts and pointed toes, plus the dropped waist line and cloche hat.'* Not everyone liked the idea, as one reader wrote to **Woman's Companion**, October 1958:

In Paris, necklines were wide, shoulders were broad, bosoms rounded and wide belts emphasised the waist. Colours included navy blue, beige and grey.

Ordinary fashions changed little. Skirts might be straight or flared. Suit jackets tended to be straight, edge to edge and waist length, either worn open or fastened with a single button at the neck, and worn with a blouse that matched the lining.

Trousers were either tight fitting and calf length, or full length, slightly fuller, with a generous turn-up. Either was worn with a chunky knit sweater or cardigan, or a shirt-type blouse. Hats were small; alternatively hair bands were popular.

Summer dresses were commonly full, knee length, shirt collared and sleeveless, with a return of the waist emphasised by a belt. A wide range of topcoats were worn: full length and flaring, fitted and belted, three-quarter length, with or without a

◀◀ A range of women's dresses, 1958.
◀ Summer dress and straw hat, 1958.
◀▼ Traditional knitted underwear was still popular, especially in the cold weather – winter draws on, as the comics would have it, though not on the BBC where the phrase was banned.
▼ A new shape is emerging: no tight waist, no padded shoulders, no thrusting bosom. As with the hairstyle, natural was becoming the operative word.

matching skirt. Popular materials were mohair, camel, tweed or wool, either in large houndstooth check, plaid or plain. Buttons were large and highly patterned or covered in matching materials.

Clothes made with Acrilan are works of art

As ever, fur was prized, either for full-length coats, jackets or stoles. Suits might have fur collars and cuffs. **Woman's Realm** advised its readers to: *'Sew an edge of fluffy fur around the hem and waistband of your favourite evening skirt.'* Or you might *'Try the flattery of a fur collar tied at the back with a velvet bow – it looks wonderful on any plain dress or sweater.'* Alternatively, *'To keep out the winds this winter, sew a face framing band of fur, or pretty fur fabric, around any plain balaclava hood.'*

◀ Tartan trousers were still the height of fashion, as were man-made fibres, Acrilan in this case.

▲ Little had changed by 1959 – skirts, straight and flared, small waists, pearl bracelet and gloves. The headbands were the latest fashion, as were the hair-styles.

# Children

*Children's clothing changed even more slowly than men's, especially school uniform, compulsory in virtually all secondary schools. Their leisure wear, though, began to veer towards that of their older siblings.*

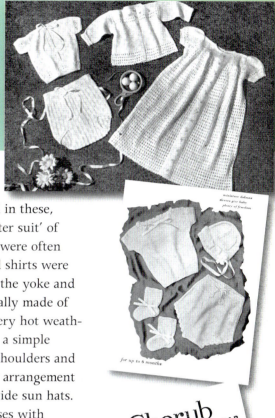

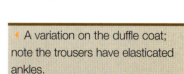

Cherub KNITWEAR

for CHILDREN

"Outgrown before Outworn"

ALSO SOCKS · UNDERWEAR · NIGHTWEAR

**The** baby's layette stayed pretty much the same as it had been for many years. The one big change was that most of it was now of man-made fibres, making it easier to clean. Dolman sleeves, or 'bat-wing' sleeves as they were often known (these are like ordinary sleeves below the elbow, but from the elbow they flare dramatically, joining the body just above the waist), were highly recommended for baby clothes, as they are much easier to put on and remove.

Toddlers, both boys and girls, had traditionally been clothed in a dress and knickers. It became far less

common for boys to be dressed in these, wearing variations on the 'buster suit' of shirt and shorts. Girls' dresses were often smocked, and both dresses and shirts were commonly embroidered across the yoke and chest. Both garments were usually made of lawn, a very fine cotton. For very hot weather girls might wear a sundress, a simple cotton dress that exposed the shoulders and upper back, and boys a similar arrangement with shorts, both worn with wide sun hats.

As they grew, summer dresses with matching knickers, both in cotton, were worn by most girls, usually with generous hems and turnings so they could be let out as the child grew. Boys continued to wear shorts, especially in the summer, though corduroy trousers, worn with jumpers, or dungarees were common wear for play, or cold weather, for either sex. Both also wore traditional tweed or wool overcoats, boys mainly wearing a cap and girls a pixie hood, although berets were not uncommon, especially for girls.

By junior school, boys generally wore a shirt (cotton in summer, flannel in winter) and tie, often a school tie. These were teamed with a jumper, almost always hand-knitted, in a wide range of styles – the V-neck slipover or sweater, cardigan or knitted, zippered windcheater being

A variation on the duffle coat; note the trousers have elasticated ankles.

Baby's layette, 1953. It had changed little over the last twenty years.

Man-made fibres proved excellent for knitting baby clothes – easy to wash and drip dry.

Tartan was particularly popular for children's clothes, even, as in this advert, for knitwear, 1958.

Knitted suit for a young toddler; many clothes for younger children continued to be handmade.

standard adult day dress, flaring from the waist to a hem worn about 6in above the knee, with a shirt collar and short sleeves, plain for normal dresses and often puffed for party versions. Other dresses had bib fronts or Tyrolean-style braces worn over a blouse or jumper. Variations included long socks and a cardigan on a cold day. Winter weather called for an overcoat, usually double breasted with a velvet collar, wellingtons and a pixie hat or beret.

Some primary school-aged girls, especially at fee-paying schools, were expected to wear a school uniform, usually consisting of a beret sporting the school badge, a school blazer, normally piped, a pleated skirt, worn short, with white ankle socks and ankle-strapped shoes. Seasonal

▲▲ Knitted swimming costume-cum-sun-suit, 1954.

▲ A cold-weather outfit featuring an interesting hat with built-in ear muffs and matching scarf.

▲ Young children celebrate the Coronation in typical summer clothes.

▶ Young girl in knitted jacket and tartan skirt. Tartan was a popular choice for such skirts.

▶▶ Swimming costume, 1952.

▼ Boy's windcheater with lots of useful pockets to keep stuff in.

the most common styles. This would be accompanied by shorts, although long trousers and even jeans with large turn-ups might be worn. Long socks were the norm, with plimsolls or sandals in summer, shoes or wellingtons in winter. Raincoats, duffle coats or overcoats would be worn in winter, with the inevit-able cap, either a school cap, or a Wolf-Cub cap.

The primary school-aged girl's day wear was the ubiquitous frock: *'lovely in velvet for special occasions, and useful in checked Dayella for everyday'*, **Woman's Weekly**, November 1952. This was worn with ankle socks and ankle-strapped shoes. In shape the dress was a close relative of the

variations included a cotton summer dress with a straw boater, bearing a badge on a band in the school colours.

The T-shirt made its appearance in the 1950s, worn much smaller than is the fashion today, along with jeans. Both were worn by girls and boys, but they were very much seen as leisure wear for the weekend or holidays.

On reaching secondary school just about everyone was expected to wear uniform. This was almost the same for boys and girls – shirt with school tie and V-necked sweater or cardigan, often worn under the school blazer. With these girls wore a gored or pleated skirt, which had to be a set length below the knee, with a school beret or soft felt hat. Long or short socks might be worn in the lower school, and in the more progressive schools sixth-form girls might be allowed stockings. In summer simple shirt-waist dresses were worn in striped or checked cotton, depending on the school rules, with the standard school cardigan. Gymslips in the school colour might still be worn for games, or Aertex shirts and huge fleecy 'games knickers', with or without a short skirt.

▲ Girls' party dresses, 1952.
◀ Typical girl's party frock with ribbon belt.
▼ A variation on the younger boy's outfit; note the long socks.
▼▼ Class photo of nine-year-olds, 1959. A wide range of typical outfits is on show (the author is at the back, second from the left).

Boys wore the standard, woollen school blazer, cap, cotton summer shirt and flannel winter shirt, with the school tie, and shorts or long trousers in flannel. In winter there would be, for both, the school scarf, worn with regulation colour raincoat or overcoat.

▶ Secondary schoolgirls' hats, 1951.
▼ Primary schoolgirl in uniform, although most did not wear uniform until secondary school.
▶ Boys secondary school uniform, 1956. Note the caps bearing the school badge.
◀ Typical girl's belted tweed over-coat, with school-type hat and long socks.

and children's socks too!

▶ Boys of several ages wearing the same outfits; the bow ties are a little formal, but otherwise they are in the uniform of all pre-teen boys.
◀ Boy and girl just about to become teenagers, when he would move into long trousers but her outfit would change very little.

# Teenagers

*In spite of all the changes in post-war fashions, the greatest revolutions that would take place in the field of dress, hairstyle, make-up, etc. was hardly visible at the start of the decade. The youth market, in the form of the teenager, would only really begin to burst onto the scene in the mid-1950s.*

**The** 1950s were a boom time for British industry, with high employment and high wages – *'You've never had it so good'*, Prime Minister Harold Macmillan famously declared, and this applied to British teenagers more than most. Of the 5 million of them in Britain in 1956, 80 per cent were working, earning incomes 50 per cent higher than their pre-war brothers and sisters had. Few had the financial commitments of their elders – mortgages, hire purchase payments, etc. – so their disposable income was high, and they spent more on clothes than anything else. The fashion trade, among others, was not slow to spot this, or to respond to it. **Vogue**, July 1955, reported that: *'Young teenagers now have a department all to themselves at Marshall and Snelgrove.'*

But they were not content to put up with what they were given, and they were not going to be dictated to by the couture houses. They wanted fashions that expressed their particular attitudes. In 1959, **Vogue** commented that: *'For millions of working teenagers clothes are the biggest pastime in life, a symbol of independence and the fraternity of an age group. The origin of the teenage look might be urban and working class, but it has been taken up with alacrity by the King's Road. It owes nothing to Paris or Savile Row; something to entertainment idols (the Tommy Steele haircut . . . the Bardot sex babe look) and much to Italy.'*

This was something altogether new. Fashions in the past, for instance, those of the mid- and late 1920s, may have been very youthful but they had never been exclusively for the young. It was, in a real sense, a revolution. Previously fashion began in Paris or London couture houses, then worked its way down to the high street. Now this was completely turned around. A few young designers in out-of-the-way shops began to create clothes, or they just seemed to evolve among groups, such as the Teds or skiffle fans, led by trend-setting members of these groups, to be

▲▲ Advert from October 1949, using the words 'Teenager' and 'Teens', although the fashions would be more young adult than anything else.

▲ Jumper for a young 'teenager', 1954.

◀◀ The **Stitchcraft** magazine of 1956, from which this comes, describes these knee-high socks as the latest teenage fashion.

◀ Teenagers in the early 1950s having good clean fun – tennis and cycling.

Young Teenager Special IN 3-PLY HERITAGE

A new Marriner design for 28, 30, 32, and 34 in. sizes. Easy to knit in "Heritage", "Halyard", "Heritage and Nylon" or "Topsail" 3 ply. Ask your Wool Shop for Marriner Leaflet 209, price 6d., or 7½d. post free from: R. V. Marriner Ltd., Dept. W.Y., Greengate Mills, Keighley, Yorkshire.

**Marriner's**

*It pays to knit with Marriner wools every time!*

At first the USA provided inspiration. In the late 1940s and early '50s, the USA, through the medium of Hollywood, was the source of all the good things that were either difficult or downright impossible to get in Britain. American magazines were full of adverts for what was, in Britain, unattainable.

The teenage girl's basic outfit consisted of a blouse and/or jumper and a simple skirt or a pinafore dress. Shaped trousers, often mid-calf level (pedal-pushers), were an alternative, worn with flat

taken up by the retail shops. The USA may have discovered the teenager, but Britain, to a large extent, developed teenage fashions.

In many ways this is not surprising. In spite of their new-found wealth, the adult world still treated them in a patronising fashion, as this advice from **Woman's Weekly**, July 1952, demonstrates: *'Arms and legs seem a bit out of control during the growing period, but the old-fashioned word "inelegant" really does apply to the sight of children, or young people, sprawling in an arm-chair. Learning to sit upright, with knees close together, is well worth the trouble, as it is going to make all the difference later on, when a young man may get his first sight of you sitting down, and either admire you, or get a general impression of clumsiness, from the attitude you have adopted.'*

Youth was creating its own fashions, and, as with most pioneers, they were not all in agreement as to the direction they should go in. Thus the variations in teenage styles were greater and more diverse than those of their parents.

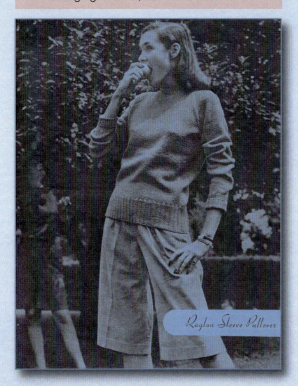

*Raglan Sleeve Pullover*

shoes or pumps (it was widely considered 'tarty' to wear high heels with slacks).

In summer girls often wore a version of the dirndl dress, either sleeveless or with small puffed sleeves. The dress was bulked out by petticoats; sometimes traditional lace-edged cotton was used, starched and ironed to add body, but more often they were of nylon, frilled or lace-edged but drip-dry and non-iron. They might even be of stiffened nylon net, when they were known as can-can petticoats, because a turn could produce a glimpse of suspenders. Originally stiffened nylon had been the sole preserve of the fashion houses, but by the late 1950s it was widely available. It was often called paper nylon as it tended to become permanently creased after a while. It was not at all uncommon to wear an older petticoat under a new

one to give skirts more body and also as an extra safeguard against showing too much leg when dancing. For dancing, especially, circular skirts that flared out were common. The outfit was completed by flesh-coloured stockings and 'winkle-picker' shoes with stiletto heels, or bobby-sox and loafers, ballet shoes, dance pumps or even baseball boots. By the late 1950s, however, the preferred 'smart' look was a high empire-line waist on a straight-cut cotton dress with cap sleeves and a round neck.

The tight jumper or cardigan became an icon of the 1950s; a polo-neck sweater or angora jumper was particularly popular with teenage girls, although twin-sets were often seen. A variation on the jumper was the loose-fitting 'Sloppy Joe', which was taken up by one group of teenagers, mainly students and/or jazz fans. At the other extreme, a female jazz fan might be seen in a leotard with a skirt. As with today, the different groups that made up what we would call youth culture often had their own particular music styles. The main ones were jazz – favoured by bohemian types, students, and what the Americans called beats, or beatniks – skiffle, an offshoot of folk, especially American folk, and rock and roll; there were, of course, some who preferred classical and other music.

By the later 1950s Brigitte Bardot had become known as 'the sex kitten'; hers was the look just about every girl aimed for; her high pony-tail began to be seen everywhere, as did her stilted, stiletto-heeled walk and her pouting, cool stare. Later the pony-tail was replaced by a short bouffant hairstyle, often worn with a headband, rather like a wide Alice band. Thus the 1950s had almost gone full swing – in August 1951, **Woman's Weekly** had recommended: *'Large coloured glass beads threaded on half a yard of millinery elastic, quite the prettiest evening head band for a young girl. The beads need not go all round, if the hair is fairly long at the back. But be sure to make a knot in the elastic at each end of the beads to prevent them slipping.'*

In the late 1940s boys had begun to take up the American 'varsity' look. Crew-cut hairstyles, worn with jeans and, most difficult to get, varsity

▶ The true teenager has emerged, 1958. Notice the Bardot-style plaits and the cool sunglasses.

▼ Plaid was a popular pattern for jumpers, skirts and trousers.

jackets – a type of flying jacket, waist length, often in satin, with elasticated waistband, cuffs and collar, in bright, college colours, with stripes along the sleeves, and a college letter or monogram on the right breast. Few could afford these things, even when they appeared in shops, but as the 1950s wore on things became easier.

One import from the USA that everyone could afford was the cinema, and in the mid-1950s, a series of films had a huge effect on Britain's youth. **The Wild One** (1953) (banned by the censor but widely talked about), starring Marlon Brando, was the story of a motorcycle gang terrorising a small town. Mild by today's standards, it was shocking at the time, fuelling fears of delinquent youth running riot, and started a fashion of motorcycle boys, later to become the Rockers, and the Hell's Angels. The following year Brando was back in **On the Waterfront** wearing a Perfecto leather jacket, T-shirt and denim jeans. **Rebel Without a Cause** (1955) bought us disturbed teenager James Dean (actually in his twenties) and his red Harrington jacket. Then in May 1956 **The Blackboard Jungle**, about a tough American high school, came to Britain. The soundtrack included Bill Haley and the Comets singing 'Rock Around the Clock' and had teenagers dancing in the cinema aisles – rock and roll had arrived! Yet another American film, **Jailhouse Rock** (1957) brought us Elvis Presley, in his third screen appearance, in denim, and this

*Plaid Pullover*

sparked an increased demand for jeans. The cinema became a symbolic centre for disaffected youth, with the newspapers full of shock stories about hooligans ripping out cinema seats.

By the mid-1950s there were other venues where different influences and music could be enjoyed by their acolytes. At jazz clubs students in over-sized sweaters and sandals, with or without duffle coats, could smoke French cigarettes and discuss surrealism. There were dance halls where girls in swing skirts and boys in sharp Italian suits jived to the new rock and roll bands. In skiffle clubs artists such as Lonnie Donegan played to fans who favoured jeans and check flannel shirts among the boys and swing skirts and blouses among the girls. Outside the cities there were coffee bars where motorcycle boys in jeans and black leather jackets and boots listened to rock on juke boxes. In the cities the new Italian espresso machines made coffee, or you could eat 'Italian rarebit', as pizza was first known, or a real hamburger in the newly arrived Wimpey bars, or a host of milk bars, ice-cream parlours and youth clubs.

This fresh American invasion, like that of 1942–5, was greeted with mixed feelings. After the war a group of upper-class men had tried to revive an English Edwardian look, wearing long single-breasted, high-buttoned, narrow-shouldered jackets with velvet collars, along with narrow trousers, a brocade waist-coat, a narrow-brimmed bowler hat, a Chesterfield overcoat and gloves. Ironically, the look was most successfully taken up by gangs of youths from London's East End in late 1953. At first they were known as 'cosh-boys' because of their favoured weapon in the many street fights that regularly took place, often with the newly arriving West-Indian immigrant community. They were the direct descendants of Mosley's blackshirts of the 1930s, and their racism and intense nationalism demanded a British fashion, and the Edwardian look was just the thing. They became the Edwardian boys or, far more commonly, the Teddy Boys or just Teds.

The fashion developed and spread widely. The long jacket became the 'drape', a thigh-length, four-button, box-cut jacket with a full back – no central seam so that it would hang better. The velvet collar extended into a unified collar and lapels, and the two flap pockets, turned-back cuffs and piped breast pocket

◀ The jive – note the swing skirts doing their stuff, 1958.

◀▼ Not all teenagers dressed in extremes, and many, indeed most, wore fairly restrained clothes such as these.

◀▼▼ Dancing in 1958 – note the long baggy jacket and trousers and the multi-layered net petticoat.

▼ The crêpe-soled shoe from 1952, adopted by the Teddy boys, who gave them the nickname of 'brothel creepers'.

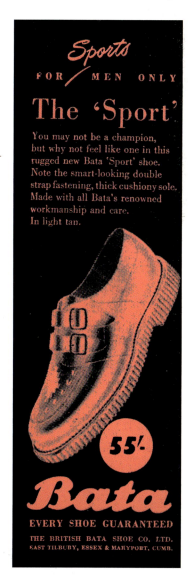

were also trimmed in velvet. To emphasise this, the main body of the coat was in a bright colour – purple, royal blue, burgundy, crimson, mustard or yellow were much favoured. A drape would cost between £30 and £100, depending on whether it was off-the-peg or made-to-measure, when the average teenager was earning around £6 a week.

Next came the extremely tight drainpipe trousers (the term had been used before for the tight trousers fashionable among women), usually in black to set off the drape. The shirt, sometimes with frilled front, was worn with a string tie or narrow 'slim-Jim' tie and the outfit was finished off with bright or even fluorescent socks, and thick crepe-soled shoes, which had become generally fashionable with men, again often of brightly coloured suede. These were known as 'beetle crushers', because of their size, or 'brothel creepers', because the crepe sole made them soundless.

The whole look was topped off by the elaborate DA haircut, where a very long fringe, heavily greased, was swept back and over the head to a little point at the nape of the neck to resemble a duck's tail. It required constant attention to keep it in place, and the enduring memory of the Teds is of a group with combs in their hands.

Teenage fashions were born in the 1950s, but they would not reach their full development until the 1960s. It is easy to fall into the trap of believing that all boys wore drapes or leathers, and all girls, tight jumpers and pedal-pushers. The reality is that, as with any age, the majority of teenagers did not

dress in the extremes that caught the eyes of the photographers, and, therefore, in retrospect, give us a false sense of the prevalence of these fashions. Most boys wore a jacket or suit in an Italian style, single breasted, narrow collared, loose fitting. Jackets were often in tweed, trousers were as narrow and shoes as pointed as your mother would let you get away with. Ties were generally slim. On cold days you wore a jumper and an overcoat, though rarely a hat. Girls were kept even more tightly controlled by their parents than boys, which would explain why their teenage fashions were more muted than their boyfriends'.

▶ Typical 1950s teenage girl – tied back hair, wide skirt and ballet pumps.

# Home Dressmaking

*'The wise girl will put aside so much a month to buy a sewing machine, which will last a lifetime and repay its cost over and over. Shoes, stockings, mackintosh and gloves one must buy, the rest can be handmade.',* **Woman's Weekly**, *September 1954.*

**Old** habits die hard, the wartime practice of 'make do and mend' became a necessity for all but the wealthiest and best connected. Continued rationing after the war reinforced this habit, and although by the 1950s rationing had gone, the habits and skills learned in the age of austerity persisted. Many women still made their own clothes, or did alterations, or knew someone who did. The home sewing machine was still put to good use.

**Woman's Weekly**, September 1954, summed it up: *'We all have the same problem nowadays: how to look well dressed and be elegant without spending too much money. The answer is really a simple one. By making our own clothes we shall be smartly turned out for less than a quarter what we would spend otherwise. Patterns today are so carefully planned and so simple to follow that we can safely trust the garments to turn out well by following instructions.'*

**Vogue**, July 1955, gave advice for the beginner: *'One of the best ways to learn is to join one of the classes organised by Singer. Apply at your local Singer Sewing Centre, and enrol for a course of eight, two-hour lessons. These are restricted to six people at a time, so that tuition is individual. Classes can be arranged for morning, afternoon or evening, and the whole course costs only 45s. (or 30s. if you are under seventeen).*

*'If you do make your own clothes, and want to acquire the couture touch of a really professional finish, dressmaker Jocelyn Richardson gives private lessons for 25s. an hour. A short course of six two-hour classes costs £8 if shared by two people.'*

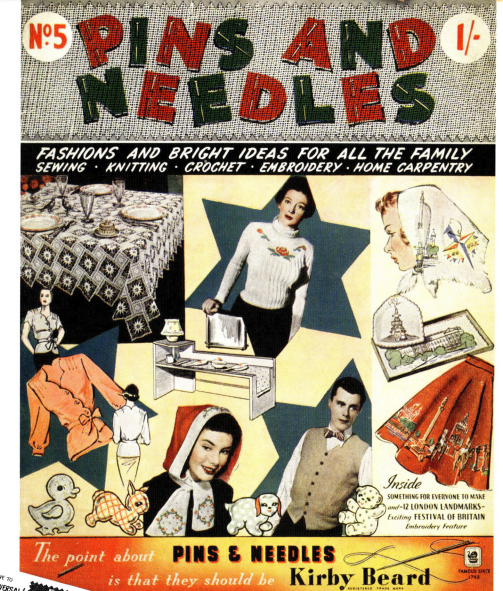

▲ This advert from 1951 shows how you could convert your treadle machine into an electric model.

▲▲ Many publications were produced to help the home dressmaker – this one is from 1951.

◀ Home dressmaking was made considerably easier by the electric sewing machine, as with this model from 1958.

## To Make a Swing Skirt

An average size of 24 inches waist and 28 inches length can be cut in one piece from 1 yard 72 inches wide heavy quality black felt; see Plan 1 (Important: If a slightly longer skirt is required, extra felt will be needed and the skirt must then be cut in two pieces and joined with two side seams. See Plan 2 which takes 40 inches of 72-inch wide felt for a skirt approx. 32 inches long.)

Coloured felts and matching cottons as follows: 6-inch square of Cardinal; 6-inch square of Pink; 6 x 5 inches of Plum; 4 x 3 inches of Bright Green; 3-inch square of Light Green. Scraps of stranded cotton in Black and Lemon. Petersham for waist, hooks and eyes, and a 9-inch zip-fastener.

To make a paper pattern for the average size – Plan 1. Take a 36-inch square of paper, measure 8 inches along top edge from one corner and 8 inches down side from same corner. Connect these by a curved line measuring 12 ½ inches (i.e., half waist plus seam allowance). Measure 28 inches outwards from this line at intervals, and mark in curved hem-line. Cut out this pattern.

Fold felt in half, place pattern on top with one straight side to folded edge and other one to cut edge of felt. Cut out carefully.

Join seam to within 9 inches of waist, taking ½ inch turnings on wrong side. Press seam flat on wrong side, but do not use a damp cloth as this will shrink the felt. Stitch petersham round waist; sew on hooks and eyes and insert zip.

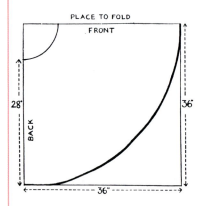

PLAN 1

the large plan shows how to cut the 28-inch length from 1 yard 72-inch felt.

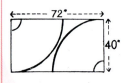

PLAN 2

for a longer skirt, follow this small plan, cutting back and front in two pieces.

# To Make a Flared Skirt, 1958

Box-pleated skirt left – Make this skirt and cummerbund from a four-yard length cut into four pieces. Make waistband and belt from the strips cut off when pattern is matched. Arrange skirt into large box pleats to waist size (about three, back and front), sew in zip, sew on waistband and neaten hem.

Dirndl skirt centre – Since you cannot cut a print like this without spoiling it, gather three or four yards tightly into a tiny waistband. In this way there is a seam down one side only. Turn up the hem and then insert a zip.

Circular skirt right – Buy four yards of fabric and cut across into two pieces. From fold edge of one piece cut a curve across from corner to corner, using a third corner as pivot. Then cut a small quarter circle from this third corner for waist. Repeat for second piece and join fabric together down the sides (seams should measure 35 in.)
Sew on waistband and hem or bind lower edge.

Pleated skirt – Buy four yards, seam up zip side and make narrow pleats starting with a 2-in. box pleat at the centre front.

**Everywoman**, June 1955, gave instructions for embroidering designs on a black net evening skirt: *'There are several ways of embroidering on net – the design can be worked from a chart or it can be tacked to the back of the net and the embroidery worked over it. Or, of course, you can work without any drawn design at all – just darn several colours through the net to form squares or diamonds. This can look most effective on black. The most important thing is that the design should be as simple as possible.*

*'Always work with a fairly blunt needle that won't catch in the mesh, and keep the back of the work neat, with all ends darned in. Should you use gold or silver thread in your design, work very carefully so that when pulling it through you do not break the mesh.'* And, in another idea to update a dress, **Woman's Companion**, November 1958, suggested: *'To give a fresh start to a taffeta dance frock, give it three silk roses – the same colour as your dress if possible – across the front of the neckline. If you are making a new dress, have the roses made of the same material. Space them out widely across the neck front.'* As the fashion for full skirts began to subside, those skirts, or rather the ample material contained within, proved excellent for remakes and renovations.

Renovations were popular. **Woman's Weekly**, August 1952, gave instructions for removing the shine from the seat of a skirt or trousers: *'mix two tablespoonfuls of cold water and two tablespoonfuls of methylated spirit with one tablespoonful of ammonia.*

*'Dip a stiff clothes brush into this solution, shake it to remove the excess moisture, then brush the shiny parts. Avoid saturating the material but brush the moisture well into it. Dip the brush into the solution frequently, and remember to shake it well each time. Finally take a piece of muslin, wring it out very tightly in the solution, place this over the shiny parts and press lightly with a hot iron.'* If, however, the skirt was worn out and was now too baggy to wear: *'make a new straight skirt in a firm navy blue material such as worsted, barathea, or suiting. Then shorten the jacket just to your hip-bone, which is the fashionable length for jackets now and bind the collar, the front fastenings and the pockets from crossways bands of the navy blue material. You will need 2 yards of 36 inch material for the skirt and bindings.'*

*'The illustration shows an effective renovation for a blouse, or dress, which is worn at the underarms. If you cannot match the material of the blouse you can use one which contrasts in texture, or in shade. For instance, a dull white crêpe could be used on a white satin blouse, or vice versa. I think that a slightly deeper, or lighter, shade of blue crêpe would look attractive on your powder blue blouse.*

*'If the worn parts beneath the arms extend over the side seams towards the back, a band of the new material the same depth as the one at the front can be added and the blouse material beneath it can be cut away.*

*'This renovation will be quite straightforward if the sleeves are removed and the side seams unpicked before the new material is added.*

*'Half a yard of 36 inch material would be sufficient to cut the front band, sleeve bands, and also a back band or collar facing. You will notice in the illustration that short sleeves have been made from the long ones. This would not be necessary if the long sleeves show no signs of wear beneath the arms.'* **Woman's Weekly**, September 1954.

**Woman's Weekly**, January 1954, suggested ways in which the *'charming wide skirt in which we square danced and went to parties all last winter'* could be brought up to date with the latest fashions: *'We suggest trimming a large patch pocket on a felt skirt with rays of sewn-on pearls, beads, or small sequins. Beads and pearls mixed look well, and the one we remember had small pearls and bronze beads on a caramel-coloured felt.*

*'Next comes the sparkling fashion for sewing large-sized paillettes of plastic nacre at intervals all over the skirt. Another pocket trim, which could as well go straight on the side of the skirt itself, is a large daisy cut from white, yellow, and green felt. The petals are white, the centre yellow, and the leaf green. Each petal should be stitched at the tip.*

> **Inexpensive fur fabric can give the same extra glamorous air {as mink} to the most simple of your dresses, coats and sweaters.'**

*'For the gathered, full, straight skirt there is nothing newer and more charming than a wide band of silk or satin ribbon stitched by machine along top and bottom edges, and finished with a large-sized flat bow at one side. The ribbon should*

contrast, or match the top. It should be placed, two-thirds of the distance from the top of the skirt to the hem.

'Rays are new, and as embroidered ribbon is a fashion as edging to blouse collars or cuffs, so it would be pretty to add the same ribbon round the waist-band, in two bands round the skirt, or as five rays from waist to hem. Coloured braid does just as well if embroidered ribbon is hard to find.

'The dotted idea is pretty when using felt as well as the paillettes. Cut out small shapes for flowers, white on green or black, blue on grey, red on green. Snip small circles for centres and sew through the circles to anchor both to the skirt in one operation. Use bright yellow felt for the centres on white flowers or red, or black – or a pearl bead. Scatter a few leaves at random. You will enjoy wearing this pretty fashion!'

**Woman's Own**, October 1953, suggested that: 'Inexpensive fur fabric can give the same extra glamorous air [as mink] to the most simple of your dresses, coats and sweaters.' While **Woman's Weekly**, August 1958, advised that: 'To give the impression of a higher waistline on an old dress, add a wide satin band, with a doubled wide sash passed under it leaving a big loop above the belt. Use dusty pink satin ribbon for a grey dress, or a printed lilac voile.'

For a navy wool dress: 'Make a white collar, shaped at the back and consisting of two ends folding in pleats to a V in front. Cut the ends neatly to fit the neck opening, and finish with a completely formal bow of two horizontal loops and two vertical ends. The bow is made of navy petersham, to show up sharply against the white

▲ Fabric-covered buttons to match the coat or dress were the latest haute-couture fashion, and *Everywoman* magazine showed you how to achieve the look.

▲▲ Children's clothes patterns, 1950.

▼ Children's clothes were always a good area for home dressmaking.

pique or linen.' And: 'If you own a black and white check suit, you are lucky, because there is nothing more becoming, more sparkling, and more fit for Spring. Give it a white collar, either a whole one or a collar back, wear with it a black sailor hat with a sea green petersham band. Under the jacket wear a black top.'

Babies' and toddlers' clothes were always a rich area for making over, and there was a myriad of advice and instructions in the women's magazines. **Woman's Companion**, November 1958, suggested: 'If the legs of your toddler's dungarees are too long, sew press studs along the turn-ups. These will hold them in place and can be removed when the legs need lengthening.' That October the magazine advised that: 'If the neck of your toddler's tee-shirt has stretched, make a slit in the ribbing at the back and insert elastic to make a firm neckline. Then sew up slit.' Or: 'If you find the little round buttons on baby's shoes won't stay done up, especially when he or she is crawling about, try replacing them with flat buttons.' Another trick with buttons was that: 'Where buttons take a great deal of "rub", such as working overalls, protect the securing thread by dabbing with a little colourless nail varnish.' This could also be used to reinforce the toes of a crawling baby's shoes; alternatively: 'a criss-cross pattern of transparent adhesive tape over the toe is helpful, too'.

**Everywoman**, March 1951, told its readers that: 'Ever since my first frock for Carol from an ex-R.A.F. shirt, friends and family have handed over to me, with a sigh of relief, literally dozens of old clothes – outmoded, gone under the arms, even moth-eaten – but "too good to

throw away" and luckily for me, good in parts. As a result, we have cupboards full of wonderful dressing-up possibilities, but we have also saved a good many pounds in the last few years over family clothes.

'Of course, you must use your discretion a bit. Big patterns and very husky fabrics look out of place on small bodies. Really worn-out material, when it goes to the washtub, makes a mockery of the time you spent on it (though a small moth-hole, hidden in fullness, can be darned).

'But the great thing about many of the materials I have unpicked has been their extraordinary quality, the like of which we can't easily buy today. Most of them wash – essential for children's things and important as anti-moth precaution if they're to be stowed away.

'I never cut down, in the sense of making a smaller version of the original garment. Children's clothes should be extremely practical (everyday) or frankly pretty (special occasions) and few grown-up things are either. So don't try to incorporate the machine-tucked bodice or the embroidered collar or whatnot into your effort. Our daughters won't thank us if they get a reputation for the home-made look.

'Instead, you must cut the original garment right up – yes, every seam must be unpicked or cut along until you have so many pieces of flat material, all shapes and sizes. When these are washed and pressed you have a better idea of what you can do.

'As the two-colour frock is rather a good idea for using up small pieces of materials, I have had it made into a pattern for you. It is a good design for remnants too, as you need only about 2½ yd. of 36-in. fabric (according to size) and ½ yd. of contrast. The frock buttons down the back (which is all in plain colour) and I placed the two pockets deliberately near the centre front, hoping they might camouflage the first spot or two that would show up so clearly on the light material.

'Of course, you know it pays time and again to sew the frock strongly. Seams won't split through wear and washing if you finish them properly with a narrow machined turn or overcasting by hand. Firmly attached collars of self material save time and

patience in upkeep. Well-cut facings behind openings and under waistbands help the garment to set nicely. You will naturally hand-sew the hem for its appearance now and easy lengthening later. And, talking of lengthening, a dress like this can err a fraction on the low-waisted side to give a good bodice line in the second year.'

Knitting was always popular. **Woman's Weekly**, September 1954, suggested that you: 'Keep a piece of knitting permanently in

hand. For taking on visits and for filling in odd moments it is ideal. You can choose the exact colour you want, too.'

**Everywoman**, March 1951, gave advice for: 'unravelling a rather tired jumper and using the wool again; undo the jumper, winding the wool,

Knitting machines were a popular way to knit quickly, and, for some, professionally.
Advert for Jaeger wool, 1958.

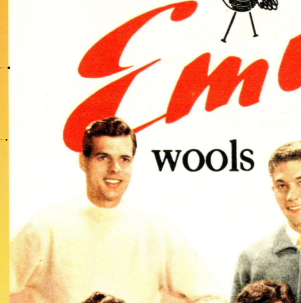

Knit with Emu wools

*section by section (back, front, sleeves, etc.), on to a fairly big book, tying each section at the top and the bottom before slipping it off the book. While you're winding, break off and throw away any wool that is frayed or thin. Wash the sections in warm, soapy water, rinse well and leave to dry. When quite dry, weigh the wool to see how many ounces you have, then find a design that requires just that amount or one that needs that amount plus an ounce or two of another colour.'*

Many knitting patterns were written on behalf of a particular wool manufacturer, and the patterns specified their wools. Was it wise to use a different make of wool from the brand quoted in knitting instructions, asked one reader of **Everywoman** in February 1958. The response was yes, provided the ply of wool was the same as the one in the instructions. But: *'Always check the tension, however, before beginning the garment, as some brands of the same ply do vary in weight and thickness. A change of needle size might be necessary to give you the right tension.'*

Again, a great deal of knitting was done for children, and so a similar amount of advice was given on the subject: *'When making woollies for fast-growing toddlers knit the ribbing twice as long, then fold in half and catch down on wrong side. Hem can be let down when necessary.'* And: *'When knitting children's woollies, make a small skein of wool and wash it each time with the woolly. When you have to darn the garment you will then have the same colour wool.'*

▲ Hand-knitted zip-up, chunky knitted windcheater for both men and women, 1958.
◀ Men's and boys' hand-knitted jumpers, 1959. A good range of styles are seen here: the knitted waistcoat and cardigan (centre) the younger style crew-neck and windcheater (rear) and the rugged chunky polo-neck.

# ACCESSORIES

## Shoes

*Stiletto heels arrived in Britain in 1953, bringing with them damage to floors and ankles. Although fashionable, they were not every woman's cup of tea.*

**The** first few years of the 1950s saw women's shoes remaining pretty much as they had been through the '40s. They were what many women described as 'clunky', with a high front (usually laced), high sides and back, wide or semi-wide medium-high heels, with a slightly pointed round toe, or in some cases open toed. Or there were low-heeled, low-fronted courts and casual shoes, with very flat soles or wedges, and a semi-high front. There were also dress and evening sandals, with a high-wedge sole, backless and open toed, with multiple straps. For beach-wear, rope-soled shoes and classic espadrilles had a continental air, or lace-up deck shoes and broad-laced 'beach ballet' shoes in striped or polka-dot denim were available.

In 1952 'Florentine' stilettos appeared in the USA, arriving in Britain in 1953. These often had markedly pointed toes. The heels caused havoc to flooring and were banned from some public buildings, while in others overshoes were provided. Some aircraft companies even complained about the harm done to airliners by them. These shoes took a lot of getting used to and there was much damage to the wearers' ankles and to the heels themselves, and heel bars offering instant repairs sprang up.

In June 1953 an advert for Bally shoes showed the 'Tracadero', an open-toed 'cocktail slipper in beautiful gold kid' with a 3¼ inch stiletto heel; the 'Garda', an open-toed sandal in jet-black suede 'with delicate pearl

▲ Advert for Styl-eez shoes, 1951. The upper shoe is very 1940s in style, while the lower model points at things to come.

overlay' and a 3in stiletto heel; and the 'Graziosa', with a 3in stiletto heel – note the Italian names. Not everyone went for the new style. Clarks shoes that summer were far more traditional with shorter, wider heels and a fully enclosed body, while K Shoes advertised flat-heeled casuals, sling-backs, peep-toe courts, wedge-soled, open-toed sandals, and Lotus promoted a wedge-soled moccasin with a high back.

Stilettos certainly did not suit everybody. They were a 'young' fashion and many teenage girls wore them (if their parents allowed them to), as high as they could get away with and preferably of the more extreme 'winkle-picker' toe variety. Women in their twenties also favoured them, but as you went up the age range, so the percentage of women wearing them went down. In July 1954, **Woman's Weekly** advised its readers to: *'Choose a good pair of black shoes with medium heels; they should be strong enough for walking and yet elegant. A court shape will stand you in good stead, perfectly plain. Your bag should team with the shoes and also be plain, and not too small.'*

**Woman's Weekly**, July 1954, recommended shoes for a summer

holiday: *'Low casual shoes can be worn for the journey, and will be perfect for the promenade, jaunts, and rambles. If you have to get a pair specially it will be worth while, and if you wear them out on the holiday the money will still have been well spent.*

*'If you go dancing, one pair of heeled slippers should be kept for this. White shoes can be temptingly different from everyday, but they have to be kept clean, so pack the wherewithal for this.*

*'For very hot places – when you are warm your feet swell, therefore it is even more important to be comfortably shod on a hot holiday, especially if you are going sight-seeing. Open mesh or open toes do let in cool draughts and are helpful.'*

◀◀ A range of K Shoes, 1953. The sandals especially are very much of the period.
▲▲ Devonshire shoes, 1958. The lower version could easily be from a decade earlier.
▲ Devonshire shoes, 1955. Many women preferred more support than the stiletto heel afforded and the majority of shoe adverts, like these, reflect this.
◀ Clarks shoes, 1953. The second from the top shows distinct 1950s styling.

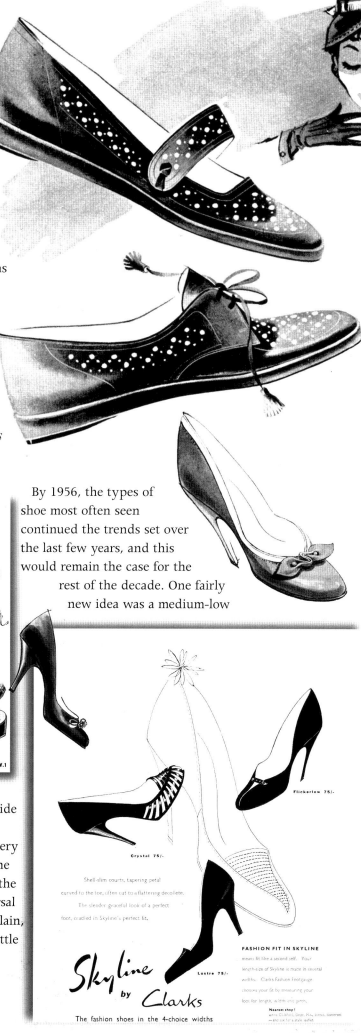

In 1955, the vast majority of shoe advertisements featured shoes that were either flat or with low or medium height heels, and most of the latter had semi-wide heels rather than stilettos. Except for the flat-heeled casuals, most were low-fronted slip-ons, with the decoration being in the form of perforations. Nearly all were semi-round toed, and summer shoes tended to be open toed. Slippers, or strapless mules, highly coloured or in gold or silver, were popular for evening wear.

Wedge-soled canvas or fabric slippers and sandals, especially embroidered versions, were very fashionable in the summer, as were Indian 'sun sandals', a kind of leather flip-flop, with decorated straps, which sold for around 25s.

Colours were often vivid thanks to the increased use of aniline dyes, but these could show rain spots. **Everywoman**, June 1955, recommended that: *'Before you wear any aniline-dyed shoes for the first time, no matter what the weather, rub them over with a good wax floor polish. It is quite a good idea to keep the shoes well waxed with floor polish always. But, please, never, never wear new shoes for the first time on a rainy day!'*

By 1956, the types of shoe most often seen continued the trends set over the last few years, and this would remain the case for the rest of the decade. One fairly new idea was a medium-low

For evening leisure and daytime pleasure

*Mimi* RECD

*Embroidered Slippers and Sandals*

Slippers obtainable in a wide range of colours, Black, Pale Blue, Pink, Gold, White and Oyster. Sandals in ten colours all richly embroidered. From Stores and leading Shoe Shops. **28/6 to 35/-**
*Send postcard for name and address of nearest retailer to*
**LIVERPOOL SHOE CO. LTD., DEPT. II, SPIRELLA HOUSE, OXFORD CIRCUS, LONDON, W.1**

▲▲▶ Flat shoes – it was not all high heels, stiletto or otherwise, in 1955.
▲▲ The long, thin heel was a development from the stiletto, 1958.
▲ Wonderful embroidered open-toed shoes for holiday wear, 1955.
▲▶ Two versions of Clarks stilettos, 1956.
▶ Clarks shoes, 1954. Stilettos had arrived, but not many women could wear them gracefully and many twisted ankles followed.

stiletto, starting wide and tapering very sharply, but also very narrow laterally, the shoe itself having the now almost universal low front, either plain, or trimmed with little bows or buckles.

Flickerlow 75/-

Crystal 75/-

Shell-slim courts, tapering petal curved to the toe, often cut to a flattering decollete. The slender graceful look of a perfect foot, cradled in Skyline's perfect fit.

Lustre 75/-

**FASHION FIT IN SKYLINE**
means fit like a second self. Your lengthsize of Skyline is made in several widths. Clarks Fashion Footgauge chooses your fit by measuring your foot for length, width and girth.

**Nearest shop!**
write CLARKS, Dept. N4, street Somerset —and ask for a style outlet.

*Skyline*
by *Clarks*

The fashion shoes in the 4-choice widths

*Autumn Aristocrats...*

for men who want smarter shoes

You get smarter styles, better workmanship and bigger values when you wear shoes by Bata. The handsome trio you see here are three of Bata's big style line for autumn. See them at your Bata dealer's before another leaf falls!

**Bata**

EVERY SHOE GUARANTEED

*Left to right—*

1. *Full brogue in tan willow with thick crepe sole.* **49/6.**

2. *Suede bold look shoe with ghillie-tie and crepe sole. Grey, brown, blue.* **49/6.**

3. *Heavy grain derby in rich tan with shaped toe-cap. Leather sole and water resistant stormwelt.* **47/6.**

*All in sizes 6-11 (half-sizes).*

THE BRITISH BATA SHOE COMPANY LIMITED, EAST TILBURY, ESSEX AND MARYPORT, CUMBERLAND

Bata shoes, 1952. The brogue (left), the suede crêpe-soled shoe that would be taken up by the Teddy boys (centre), and a very interesting buckled affair (right).

which a lot of men wear with business suits nowadays? It started life as a very rugged shoe for the Scotsman to wear with his kilt. Then it came south of the border for golf, became a smart, all-purpose country style in tan, from which the town shoe evolved.

'Another country shoe that has come to town in the same way is the mudguard style, starting off with the familiar apron-fronted shoe; the sides of the upper in this particular style seem to have moved down closer to the welt, thus making the "mudguard" that extra half-inch or so of protection that runs around just where the sole joins the upper.'

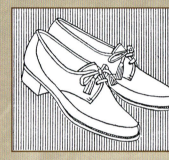

On holiday, men might be a little more daring, wearing plimsolls, deck shoes, espadrilles or even sandals, though usually with socks.

At home, of course, carpet slippers were worn, either traditional style or one of the new types available. **Men Only**, December 1955, suggested: 'For the man who wants something not only good but out of the ordinary, let me mention the idea of genuine hand-made North African slippers. They're made of tough but supple leather and are styled to a distinctive wedge shape. Soles are of laminated leather. The heel flap can be worn up, to grip in the usual way; or down, for a looser, push-on fit. 37s. 6d.

'There are two other sorts of slippers which are as attractive in their way. The first sort is in camel-suede with a sheerling (lambswool) lining. This slipper has a classic Grecian styling with super-flexible leather soles. It retails at approximately 35s. The second is a travelling slipper made of a super-supple scarlet leather. The slippers fold flat and clip together with a band. They have very soft leather soles and retail for approximately one guinea.'

Like most male fashions, shoes changed very slowly over the decade. As with women, teenagers found their own, often radical, new fashions and these included the baseball boot and the 'winkle picker', not actually one sort of shoe, but a whole range, the important thing being the pointed toe, the more pointed the better. They were even more desirable in an unusual material, such as suede or crocodile skin.

As with women's shoes, however, these more daring styles were limited to the young. For older men fashion was more restrained. Writing in **Men Only**, November 1955, Humphrey Savile asked: *'Do you like to see the smart, black town brogue shoe*

MEN'S SANDALS

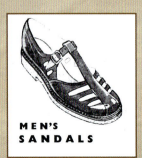

NORVIC
**Flitemasters**
get your feet off the ground!

# Socks & Stockings

*'Coloured woollen stockings have come to town! They are so warm, so gay and we think at least one pair in a young girl's wardrobe is a 'must'. Just imagine yourself twinkling along wearing stockings of royal blue, kingfisher green, hunting red or guinea gold. Or, if you would like this better, in neutral or black'*, **Woman's Weekly**, *March 1959*.

Like cosmetics, the war had seen stockings, and especially nylons, virtually disappear, with almost the only sources being the black market or American GIs. With the end of clothes rationing the demand for stockings boomed.

Nylon, a synthetic material made from a mixture of coal and water, had first been produced in the late 1930s and was used to make a whole range of things, especially clothing, but it was so good for making sheer stockings that the name 'stockings' was virtually superseded by 'nylons'. By 1953 service weight (hard-wearing), stretch nylon stockings were available. Very sheer, moulding themselves to the leg rather than wrinkling, and far less likely to ladder, they were a huge advance in the manufacture of stockings.

*Always look for the name*

There were several types and grades of stocking depending on their use and durability: everyday, evening wear etc., described by gauge and denier. In 1953, Taylor-Woods described what the various types meant: *'Gauge is the number of stitches in each 1½ inches and the higher the gauge number the stronger the stocking. Denier is the thickness of the yarn; the lower the denier number, the finer the stockings.'*

Then followed a list of the various stockings they produced:

*54 gauge 30 denier – Service weight for everyday wear*

*54 gauge 15 denier – Very sheer for evenings and special occasions*

*66 gauge 15 denier – Semi-service, semi-sheer for day and evening wear*

By 1955 they had added:

*66 gauge 12 denier – A luxury version of 66 gauge*

*75 gauge 12 denier –*
*Strongest of all sheer nylons – the gift deluxe*
Other suppliers also produced 66 gauge 30 denier which were described as weekend wear, and 51 gauge 12 denier 'for special occasions'.

As well as different types, they also came in various colours. In February 1954, **Woman's Own** informed its readers that: *'Accent goes to the legs and feet with the shorter skirt, and pastel-coloured nylon stockings are the prettiest things we've seen for some time. Colours are picked to match your party dress or important outfit. Wear evening slippers to match for that expensive look. Price 10s. 3d.'*

In 1955 sheer stretch nylons arrived in Britain. They were marketed as sheer but hard-wearing; perhaps the adverts over-stressed the hard-wearing side, giving

Stockings, for so long an object of almost unattainable desire under rationing, were now back on the market.

*look enchanting in*

**MORLEY**
*nylons*

rise to unwarranted expectations, and they came in for a lot of criticism from certain quarters. **Charnos**, the maker of *'Sheers-t-r-e-t-c-h'* nylons, tried to put matters right. In one advert, in February 1956, they pronounced that: *'Sheers-t-r-e-t-c-h nylons have far more give-and-take and so are less liable to overstrain – one of the main causes of stocking "runs". However, if you give s-t-r-e-t-c-h a tough time when you put them on and take them off you are inevitably in for trouble! For although they have long-wearing properties the fact remains that no sheer nylons can stand up to rough handling – and s-t-r-e-t-c-h are no exception to this rule.'* They went on to explain how to get the most from stockings: *'Never wear stretch nylons for more than one day without washing them. When putting on, always gather the stocking very gently in your hands before easing it over your foot, avoiding as far as possible all contact with finger nails. Take a little extra trouble to fit the heel snugly – this is well worthwhile as you will always get perfect fit with stretch give-and-take. Draw the stocking smoothly up your leg, guiding the seam. See that it is evenly stretched all the way up from the heel. Once straight, your stretch seams stay straight all day long.'*

In spite of this nylons continued to run. However, you could have your nylons invisibly mended. One advert in **Vogue**, July 1955, offered a 24-hour service at a cost of 1s 9d per stocking for: *'any number of ladders, holes etc.'*

**Woman's Companion** magazine of November 1958 pointed out that it was important to get your right stocking size for comfort and wear, and described how this should be done: *'Stand on a piece of paper, draw the outline of your foot, then measure this from toe to heel. This will give you your*

correct stocking size, without guessing.'

Yet it wasn't just the fact that they ran that made many women dislike wearing stockings, as one reader of **London Life** magazine wrote, in May 1958: *'I detest wearing suspender belt or garters in the warm weather and yet I don't like to go without stockings. Can you tell me of any way of keeping hose up without suspendering or gartering them?'* The suggested solution was to run a double length of elastic through the tops of your stockings, giving a built-in garter that did not show. Alternatively: *'you can do what some model girls do, which is coat the inside of the top part of your nylons with quick drying varnish, and while they are still wet, stick them to your legs, and the hose will keep in place and not twist or turn. Mind you, it's not a comfortable device, and the varnish might make the skin sore if you use this trick regularly.*

*'If you don't like either idea, the answer seems to be to paint your legs with sun-tan and go without stockings altogether.'*

## Socks

As with much else, man-made fibres began to dominate the sock industry. Men were famously conservative in their dress, with change happening only very slowly, and these new materials were seen by some as almost revolutionary.

In 1952, **Men Only** advised its readers that: *'Socks made from a fifty-fifty blend of wool and nylon are now well recognised as being no less comfortable than an all-wool sock, though very much harder-wearing, to the extent of providing months of extra wear before there is any need for darn-*

**Instal a DD machine**

HOSIERY REPAIRING

**and profit by OUR experience**

Repair laddered Hosiery and Earn Money. Ideal Home business. The only all-British Equipment. Hire purchase terms available from 12/- weekly.

*Free tuition and details from*

**DOROTHY DEAN LTD.**

89 High Street, Wealdstone, Middx. Phone : Harrow 3131

Dimensions: 8" at base × 11" high

DHB

At last! Comfort and elegance with **Pretty Polly** TRU-SUPPORT STOCKINGS

Do you suffer from weary legs and feet? A tendency to varicose veins? Are you a mother to be? Then here's wonderful news! Pretty Polly have perfected for *you* a new-type support stocking with a fully-fashioned-nylon look. TRU-SUPPORT stockings are made on the latest type of fully-fashioned machines from a clever combination of crepe nylon and rubber. They'll keep you both comfortable and fashionably dressed.

Obtainable in medium and full widths in each foot size for perfect fit; in shades of Pecan Beige, Mentone and Daytaupe.

*only* 39/6 *pair*

▲▲ Today no one would dream of mending laddered tights, but that was not the case in the 1950s.

▲ Support stockings were available to those who needed them.

▶ The fashion in men's socks was still calf length, 1956.

◀ Man-made materials meant that the old sock suspenders, while still available, became old fashioned.

Don't pull your socks up ! Wear **Sphere** Wear BROADWAY SUSPENDERS

"SPHERE" SUSPENDERS, BRACES, BELTS AND GARTERS STAND PRE-EMINENT

**GRIP-EEZI** THE ORIGI... SELF-SUPPORTING SOCKS for **MEN** and...

(A Paramount (Regd...

For quality and all round... there can be nothing fi... Lastex garters prevent s... wrinkles. Pure botany... nylon reinforced heels... strength and long we...

Remember also... source, "PARA... Outerwear. Ask... good outfitter... them, please...

TOWLES LTD. L...

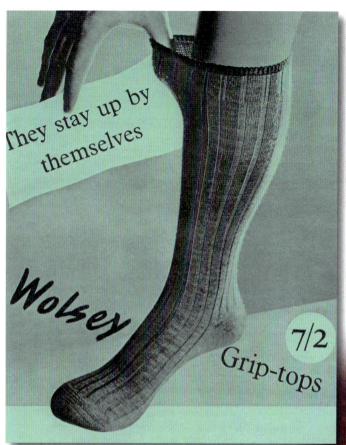

They stay up by themselves

*Wolsey*

7/2

Grip-tops

*ing. These socks are available from various shops up and down the country. This long-life sock costs 6s. 9d.'*

However, the change in men's attitudes took time as illustrated by one reader of **Men Only** who wrote, in November 1955: *'Before I invest in socks in nylon or Terylene, have they any effect on foot comfort? And for or against? . . . Yes, there are slight differences compared with most wool socks. First, the synthetics are usually just that much finer and closer-fitting, which tends to make the shoe fit a little easier; next, there is less elasticity, which means you should make more sure to get your sock size right.'*

One month later, the same magazine was advising women on Christmas gifts for men: *'A lot of men welcome socks, too, but until lately the styling and the size have presented too much of a problem. The lady-friend can hardly be faulted, however, if she chooses crimped-nylon socks. They not only provide a new and altogether pleasing foot sensation, but she is sure to buy the*

*right size because they S-T-R-E-T-C-H. The colours are simple, too, so men will not be frightened to go about in them!'*

The ability to stretch, which, unlike wool, did not disappear after a couple of washes, meant that they would stay up, without the need for sock suspenders, and the use of these rapidly declined.

▼ Man-made fibres meant thinner, better-fitting socks, in a new range of colours, to fit the post-war mood.

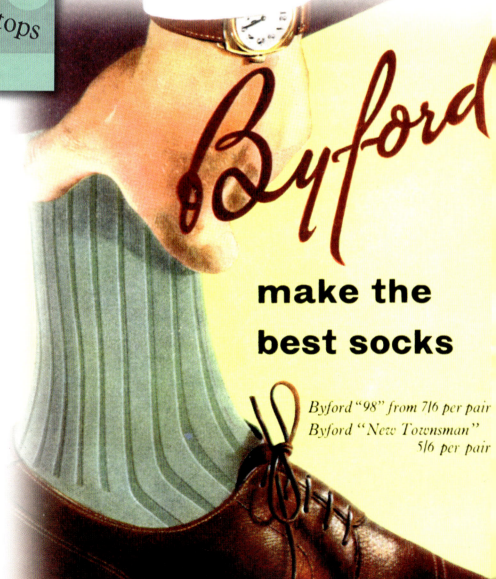

*Byford*

**make the best socks**

*Byford "98" from 7/6 per pair*
*Byford "New Townsman" 5/6 per pair*

# Hats

*'Wear your coat to one of the big chain stores where there are counters crammed with hats at a very modest price. Stand in front of a mirror showing your whole length if possible, and don't get anything big to make you look heavy at the head.'* **Woman's Weekly**, July 1954.

Chic from every angle

KANGOL

In the 1950s women wore hats in an assortment of sizes, styles and materials, so that in the same street you would see large straw hats, tiny pillboxes with nets and the whole range of sizes and materials in between. What was stressed by the magazine fashion gurus was the need to wear a hat that suited your shape, or your outfit, or your hairstyle. For example, with the short gamine haircut, very small or very large hats were to

▲ A range of Kangol hats, 1956.
▶ A pillbox hat with flower, 1954.
▼ A rather striking hat, 1953.

be worn, whereas the chrysanthemum cut had to be worn with a Cossack or other drum-shaped hat.

Tall women were advised to wear big-brimmed, wide-crowned hats, small women, small hats but with an up-swept line, heavy women, hats that stressed height, with substantial brims with a sufficient feeling of width to balance wide hips, and so on. Added to this were the seasonal variations. In the autumn and spring hats tended to be small, such as the pillbox or the saddle hat, which, as its name suggests, was a

sort of curved oval shape, fitting the top of the head rather like a saddle. Summer hats were far bigger, and the recurring oriental theme in fashions meant that a straw coolie hat was always acceptable.

Berets, worn in a flat, pancake shape, were common before 1955. **Woman's Weekly**, January 1952, suggested that: *'Endless variations can be rung on your faithful friend the round muffin beret. Try trimming it with fancy braid arranged in a square on the round surface, twisting the braid to give extra emphasis at each corner. Black braid on an emerald green beret, white on black, puce on royal blue, black on brown or caramel.'*

## To Knit a Ribbed Stocking Cap (to fit Average Head) [1954]

<u>Materials:</u> Four balls of fine ply. A set of four number 12 needles pointed both ends. 1 yard of black bobble fringe.

<u>Tension:</u> 10 sts to an inch over rib patted out flat.

N.B. use wool double throughout.

With the set of four No. 12 needles, cast on 160 sts (53, 54, 53). Work in rib thus:

1ST ROUND: *p. 3, k. 2; repeat from * to end. Repeat this round for 3 inches. Now reverse brim thus:

NEXT ROUND: *k. 3 p. 2; repeat from * to end. Repeat this round until piece measures 7 inches from start. Here start to shape top:

NEXT ROUND: * k. 1, k. 2 tog., p. 2, k. 3, p. 2; repeat from * to end (144 sts).

NEXT ROUND: * k. 2, p. 2, k. 3, p. 2; repeat from * to end. Repeat last round for a further 4.5 inches.

NEXT ROUND: * k. 2, p. 2, k. 1, k. 2 tog., p. 2; repeat from * to end (128 sts).

NEXT ROUND: * k. 2, p. 2; repeat from * to end. Repeat last round for a further 3 inches.

NEXT ROUND: Rib 2 tog., rib 60 (rib 2 tog.) twice, rib 60, rib 2 tog. (124 sts). Work 1 round straight keeping continuity of rib.

NEXT ROUND: Rib 2 tog., rib 58 (rib 2 tog.) twice, rib 58, rib 2 tog. (120 sts). Work 1 round straight.

NEXT ROUND: Rib 2 tog., rib 56 (rib 2 tog.) twice, rib 56, rib 2 tog. (116 sts). Work 1 round straight.

Continue thus, decreasing 4 sts. On next and every alternate round until 60 sts remain, then decrease 4 sts on every round until 24 sts remain. Divide sts evenly on two needles and graft.

Do not press. Fold brim up twice and sew bobble fringe behind. Make two deep pleats round top of hat and sew in position with matching sewing cotton, or alternatively twist round and secure with pearl hat pin.

## To Crochet a Puffball Beret (to fit Average Head) (1954)

*Materials:* Either 1oz. fingering 3-ply and 1oz. angora, or 2oz. angora. No. 10 crochet hook, cotton wool for padding.

*Tension:* 5 d.c. with 5.5 rows to an inch. Fingering and angora used together or double angora.

Begin at centre crown. Make 4 chain, join into a ring with a slip stitch. Continue as follows:- 8 d.c. in centre of ring, join with a slip stitch. * 1 d.c. in 1 d.c., 2 d.c. in 1 d.c. *; rep. From * to * until crown measures 2 inches across. Continue thus:- ** (1 d.c. in 1 d.c.) 7 times, 2 d.c. in 1 d.c. **; repeat from ** to ** until crown measures 4 inches across.

Continue thus:- *** (1 d.c. in 1 d.c.) 10 times, 2 d.c. in 1 d.c. ***; repeat from *** to *** until crown measures 6 inches across. Mark the last stitch with coloured cotton. Now work straight in d.c. for 25 rounds from coloured thread. Fasten off.

Cut a piece of cotton wool 10 inches long and 3 inches wide. Fold into three lengthways. Place inside hat brim at front and fold crochet brim over twice, allowing sides of brim to slope away to full depth at back. Catch down at intervals on wrong side. Cut a circle of cardboard 5.5 inches across, place inside hat, then press crown on wrong side with warm iron and damp cloth. Remove cardboard.

▲ A halo cap, a variation on the saddle hat, 1953.
▶ A wide-brimmed felt hat, 1953.

# HATS TO SUIT YOUR FACE

## For a Square Face

*A beret type hat balances a square chin; avoid anything at all masculine-looking. The simple styles suit you.*

## A Heart-shaped face

*Lucky you, hats look divine on you. Even the high-fashion cone which hides your hair. Beware of anything too large, though.*

## For an Oval Face

*No droopy hairstyles or sweeping feathers for you. The modified headache band is still in fashion, and you can wear it.*

## For a Round Face

*Watch out, it can be irritation to be called "baby-face"! A smooth hairstyle will give you dignity. (Small picture shows how the back of a French Knot should look.)*

There's something about a sailor . . . and here in Swiss Fancy Straw is a sailor that has 'something' . . . Choose it in Black, Navy, White, Carbon Grey White or in Burnt, and wear it with confidence for many occasions in this wonderful Coronation Season. You can buy Model 06961 at leading milliners and stores for approximately 49 -. Headfitting 6¾

*Woolsand*

GREAT MARLBOROUGH STREET, LONDON, W.1

*'Have you a pudding basin shape hat? Remove any ribbon band or other trim, and find or buy several sprays of small flowers such as lilac or mimosa. If necessary divide the sprays so that the effect is light and airy. Stitch (with only a catching thread here and there) a few sprigs round the top of the crown and a few sprigs round the base of the crown. Lilac round a white hat looks enchanting. Save a few of the flowers to tuck into the waist of your dress, or the lapel of your suit',*

**Woman's Companion**, November 1958.

As with men, it became more common to see women going hatless by the end of the decade, although not nearly to the same extent.

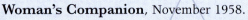

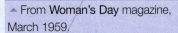

▲ From **Woman's Day** magazine, March 1959.

▲▲ ▶ A hand-knitted beaded cap, 1955.

▲ A straw hat, 1953.

▶ Kangol berets, 1955. Berets, with their continental feel, were very popular, especially the 'Muffin'.

◀ Pillbox hat with veil, 1953.

MUFFIN

PIKIBERET
Reg. Des. Patent pending

Chic from every angle

ANGLOBASQUE

**KANGOL**

THE FASHION BERET

Cleator / Cumberland

# A Crocheted Sunday Hat

<u>Materials</u>: 4oz. macramé twine No. 10. No. 10 crochet hook; 43 in. millinery wire.

<u>Tension</u>: from side to side of 1 group measures about 1 inch, 1 row measures ¾ inch.

Start at centre crown. Make 5 ch., join into a ring with a slip stitch (s.s.).

1st round: 9 d.c. through centre of ring, join with s.s.

2nd round: 5 ch. (this counts as 1 dbl. tr. at beg. of round), 1 dbl. tr. into 1st d.c., 2 ch., 2 dbl. tr. into same st., * 2 dbl. tr. in next d.c., 2 ch., 2 dbl. tr. in same st. (this makes 1 group; repeat from * to end, s.s. into 5th of 5 ch. (9grs.).

3rd round: s.s. along to sp. in centre of 1st group, (5 ch., 1 dbl. tr., 3 ch., 2 dbl. tr.) all into sp., *(2 dbl. tr., 3 ch., 2 dbl. tr.) into sp. in centre of next gr., repeat from * to end, s.s. into 5th of 5 ch.

4th round: s.s. along to sp. in centre of gr. (5 ch., 1 dbl. tr., 3 ch., 2 dbl. tr.), into sp., *(2 dbl. tr., 3 ch., 2 dbl. tr.) all into top of 1st dbl. tr. of next gr. (2 dbl. tr., 3 ch., 2 dbl tr.), all into sp. in centre of next gr.; repeat from * to end, join with s.s. into 5th of 5 ch. (18 grs.).

5th round: s.s. along to sp. in centre of gr. (5 ch., 1 dbl. tr., 3 ch., 2 dbl. tr.), into sp., *(2 dbl. tr., 3 ch., 2 dbl. tr.), all into sp. in centre of next gr.; repeat from * to end, join with s.s. into 5th of 5 ch.

6th round: s.s. along to sp. in centre of gr. (5 ch., 2 dbl. tr., 3 ch., 3 dbl. tr.), into sp., *(3 dbl. tr., 3 ch., 3 dbl. tr.) all into sp. in centre of next gr.; repeat from * to end, join with s.s. into 5th of 5 ch.

7th – 9th rounds: as 6th.

10th round: s.s. along to sp. in centre of gr. (5 ch., 1 dbl. tr., 3 ch., 2 dbl. tr.), into sp., *(2 dbl. tr., 3 ch., 2 dbl. tr.) all into top of 1st dbl. tr. of next gr. (2 dbl. tr., 3 ch., 2 dbl. tr.), into sp. in centre of next gr.; repeat from * to end, join with s.s. into 5th of 5 ch. (36 grs.).

11th – 12th rounds: as 5th round.

13th – 14th rounds: as 6th.

15th round: 1 s.s. into each stitch and each ch. All round; fasten off.

Using four thicknesses of remaining twine, crochet a chain and slot through spaces of 9th round, finishing ends with bobbles. With matching cotton sew wire to last round of brim on wrong side.

# Men

One of the biggest changes in men's clothing over the decade was hats. At the start of the 1950s few men would have felt properly dressed outside without a hat, be it a Homburg, trilby or flat cap – all very traditional styles. In 1952, **Men Only**'s clothes writer placed hats in the first stage of what a man needed in his basic wardrobe: *'If your general outerwear is limited, you can at least bolster up the impression of greater variety by varying the accessories. Thus I'd have a sporty-looking, rough-surfaced soft felt in, say, a mixture-colour green, for informal wear; and a clean-cut snap brim felt in, say, medium blue-grey, to give a more dressy atmosphere in town. With the clothing so far available, it obviously wouldn't be possible to overdo the formality of any accompanying accessories. One wouldn't, for instance, make the second hat a black Homburg.'*

By December 1955, his recommendations were more sporty, reflecting the general fashion trend towards leisure clothing: *'For any outdoor leisure occasion – golf, walking, motoring, sports-spectating, a man can find good use for one of those lightweight one-piece pure wool caps which are so popular nowadays. The same softness which gives the cap so much of its comfort also enables it to be slipped into the pocket when not being worn, without losing its freshness of finish. At 10s. 6d., these caps are made in sizes from 6¾ to 7½, and in no fewer than 18 colours.'*

The bowler made a brief return as part of the Edwardian revival, which itself transformed into the Teddy-boy style, although the bowler hat was not adopted as part of this. Generally, it was not the habit of teenage boys to wear a hat. This remained the case throughout the 1950s, and, as teenage fashions were to influence heavily, first, younger adult fashions and then work their way upwards, being hatless gradually spread so that by the end of the decade few men would be seen wearing a hat in any but the worst of weathers.

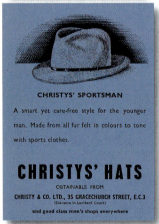

▲▲ The 'Tyrone' man's beret, 1955. These never really caught on as they reminded men too much of National Service.

▲ The traditional men's trilby style hat, still going strong in 1952.

▲ The beret cap, a variation on the traditional flat cap, smaller and less rigid, designed to be folded up and kept in the pocket when not in use.

▼ Another variation on the flat cap, previously considered very working class but now seen as rather sporty.

# Gloves

*'What smart woman can see the season through without three or four pairs of crocheted gloves?',* **Coats** advert, February 1954.

▲ White gloves, the perfect accompaniment to the summer dress.

**Gloves** were an important feature of most women's outfits in the 1950s. Long gloves in silk, or lace, for formal wear; leather, suede or wool gloves for cold weather; little white cotton gloves for parties, or a girl's first dance; and crocheted gloves for general going out.

## To Crochet a Pair of Woman's Gloves to Fit an Average Hand

Tension: 6 half trebles to an inch on No. 12 hook.

Both hands alike. Begin at side edge. With No. 12 hook, make 41 chain, turn.

1st row: miss 1 ch., * 1 half treble in 1 ch.; repeat from * to end, turn with 2 ch.

2nd row: * 1 h.tr. in 1 h.tr.; repeat from * to end; break cotton and rejoin at other end.

Next row: 25 h.trs in 25 h.trs., 19 ch. for 3rd finger, turn. **

Next row: * 1 h.tr. in 1 stitch; repeat from * to end, turn with 2 ch. Repeat last row twice more. **

Next row: 25 h.trs in 25 h.trs., 21 ch. for middle finger, turn. Rep. From ** to ** once.

Next row: 25 h.trs in 25 h.trs., 19 ch. for 1st finger, turn. Rep. From ** to ** once.

Next row: 19 h.trs in 19 h.trs., 14 ch. for thumb, turn.

Next row: 14 h.trs in 14 ch., 7 h.trs in 7 h.trs., 1 slip-stitch in next stitch, turn; 21 h.trs in 21 h.trs., turn.

Next row: 24 h.trs in 24 h.trs., 1 ss. in next stitch, turn.

Next row: * 1 h.tr. in 1 h.tr.; repeat from * to end. Fasten off.

Work 1 row double crochet down side of thumb and all round fingers, ending at top of little finger. Now work down side of little finger to wrist thus: -

Next row: * 1 h.tr. in 1 h.tr.; repeat from * to end, turn with 2 ch. Rep last row 4 times more.

*** Next row: 12 d.c. in 12 h.trs., 13 h.trs.. in 13 h.trs., 19 ch. turn.

Next row: 32 h.trs in 32 sts., 12 d.c. in 12 d.c.

Next row: 12 h.trs.,.. in 12 d.c. * 1 h.tr. in 1 h.tr.; repeat from * to end.

Next row: * 1 h.tr. in 1 h.tr.; repeat from * to end. ***

Next row: 12 d.c. in 12 h.trs., 13 h.trs.. in 13 h.trs., 21 ch. for middle finger, turn.

Next row: 34 h.trs in 34 sts., 12 d.c. in 12 d.c.

Next row: * 1 h.tr. in 1 st.; repeat from * to end. Repeat last row once. Now repeat from *** to *** once.

Next row: 12 d.c. in 12 h.trs., 7 h.trs. in 7 h.trs. 14 ch., turn.

Next row: 14 h.trs. in 14 ch., 7 h.trs. in 7 h.trs. 1 ss. in next stitch, turn.

Next row: 21 h.trs. in 21 h.trs., turn.

Next row: 24 h.trs. in 24 h.trs., 1 ss. in next stitch, * 1 d.c. in 1 d.c.; repeat from* to end.

Next row: 1 h.tr. in 1 stitch to top of thumb. Finish off by working a row of d.c. down side of thumb and all round fingers, ending at top of little finger; fasten off. Make another glove in the same way.

To Make Up: Press parts carefully on wrong side under a damp cloth. Join sides and fingers remembering to turn second glove inside out for other hand. With No. 13 hook, begin at side edge and work 1 row d.c. round wrist edge, turn with 1 ch. Work 7 more rows in d.c., then 1 row of slip-stitches, working these round side openings as well. With 6 strands of black cotton, work saddle-stitching around cuff.

By 1958, most gloves came in the obligatory synthetic fibres. **Woman's Weekly** advised that: *'Gloves which are longer length are elegant enough to give an air to any outfit. Made of the best nylon, they are wearable in light shades winter and summer; they dry overnight, so establish a habit of being ready with clean gloves every time you go out on any sort of formal occasion.'*

Even by the end of the 1950s, when the more informal, casual look was fashionable, in the summer many women would still wear white, cotton gloves with a bright-patterned, cotton or synthetic dress.

## Men

A reader of **Men Only** magazine asked in December 1955: *'Can you suggest a kind of glove which will give most warmth with least bulk? I have tried a leather glove with a chamois lining, and didn't think it was warm enough.'* The reply was: *'Probably that was because it fitted too well. A close-fitting glove usually seems to have little warmth. Warmest*

gloves are those with fur or cropped-lamb lining, but they are more bulky. For neatness, with adequate-to-good warmth, you would do best with an unlined pair of heavy chamois gloves, a half-size easier (larger) than usual.'*

The same magazine, in November 1952, commented that: *'One doesn't have to be particularly ancient to remember the days when any reasonably well-dressed man used gloves not only for warmth in winter, but for convention's sake, all through the summer. (It was only thirteen years ago, after all.)'* They were, of course referring to pre-war 1939. The article continued: *'Now, of course, men are much more logical than conventional, and anybody wearing or carrying gloves with a lounge suit would certainly attract a second glance.*

*'But are we really so logical about this matter of glove-wearing? I'm inclined to doubt it. Most men wear in winter a glove which is altogether too heavy for their real needs. Instead of the old transition from*

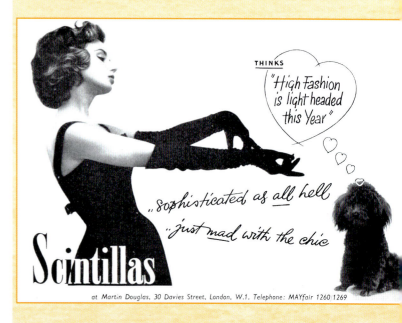

milord

*The most Beautiful Gloves in Fashion*

a summer-weight chamois to a winter-weight tan Cape leather, with a wool lining as likely as not, the usual change nowadays is from nothing to the same old gloves as of yore.

'Mostly it's just habit, plus the unconscious assumption that a lighter-weight glove couldn't possibly be warm enough for winter.

'Certainly an overcoat worn without gloves doesn't look right. It has a sort of raw, unfinished effect. Therefore, a man normally goes into glove-wearing at the same time as he resumes his overcoat – with the first cooler days of autumn. It seems hardly logical to wear at that moment the same kind of gloves as would be adequate for the depths of winter.

'If I may quote from my own experience, I happen to have a pair of substantial tan leather gloves lined with a close-cropped lamb's wool – a present, of course. They're quite a typical kind of good winter glove in the eyes of the trade, yet I don't suppose I've worn them more than half a dozen times in the past three winters together, simply because I find (to my surprise) that the lighter-weight gloves with which I start the autumn somehow continue to prove adequately warm through virtually all the winter.'

With the general trend towards leisure-based clothing for men, and the arrival of the nippy small sports car, driving gloves appeared, to go with the small peaked cap, check sports jacket and cravat. Nowadays, this ensemble is almost seen as a stereotype, but then it was definitely a look.

◄▲ Most women wore gloves on formal occasions and many wore them whenever they went out.
◄▼ Very 'sophisticated' long gloves, Scintillas 1953.
▼ Men's knitted gloves.
▼ Men's suede and leather gloves.

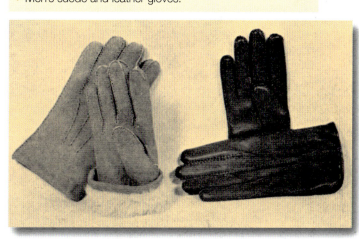

# Belts

*The belt became an increasingly important piece of clothing as the waist became the central focus of the hourglass female figure.*

▸ Belts were worn, even over jumpers, to emphasise the fashionably small waist.
▸▸ Two DIY belts, 1958.
▾ Suggestions for belts, 1958.

Belts were used to accentuate the waistline, and a bright belt drew attention to a small waist.

Alternatively, those whose waist measurement left something to be desired, even with the aid of a formidable foundation garment, were strongly advised not to draw attention to it, omitting a belt altogether.

At the start of the 1950s belts were one of the items of female dress that were most often home-made. **Woman's Weekly**, August 1951, suggested that: *'You may like to embroider a design in ordinary garden bast on a strip of dark wool material to make yourself a belt. It's amusing and straightforward work as there are no colours to confuse, and the effect, especially on black, is good and very "different". Choose a fairly bold design and use the bast in a medium width, stripping the strands to suit as you go and using a crewel needle with a big eye. When finished, you can send the strip to be backed, buckled and finished at a stitchery-and-belt-making shop.'* The last sentence is a fascinating glimpse into shops in the post-war period!

In 1952, tight bodices were the fashion and this could be achieved without the expense of a new dress by the simple means of a cummerbund. **Woman's Weekly** that year advised its readers that: *'If you are making your own skirt, save enough material for a cummerbund. You must be careful however, as it will not be enough just to gather the material into folds – as this will simply fill in your waist curve. You must lay the belt out and machine it into [horizontal] pleats, press them flat and mount on to a petersham, with fastening and buttons, to complete.*

*'A pleated silk or satin belt to tone with the skirt is another way of dealing with the all-important waistline. The front part can be fully rucked and wide while the back can be quite plain, or tapered to a fastening. Tack the silk into folds and mount it on scrim.'* Alternatively, a contrasting cummerbund, such as yellow velvet on a black dress, was recommended.

In 1953, the Coronation year, jewellery was all important. **Woman's Own**, in October 1953, advised that: *'Ordinary shirt buttons and tiny brilliants are all*

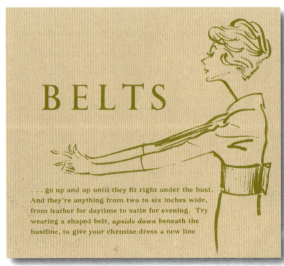

BELTS

. . . go up and up until they fit right under the bust. And they're anything from two to six inches wide, from leather for daytime to satin for evening. Try wearing a shaped belt, *upside down* beneath the bustline, to give your chemise dress a new line

the decoration you need to make a really smart belt.'

By 1954, **Woman's Weekly** recommended: 'When finishing a slim, straight frock, have a change from an ordinary belt, and make instead a wide sash. All you need is a six-inch strip, which is turned in with the tiniest seams along each side. At each end, machine a strip of furnishing fringe – white, red, or black, according to the accent you prefer. It will give just the telling touch which needs no other addition.'

The new man-made materials were just the thing for belts. Many bright, plastic belts were on sale, in various widths normally from $1/2$ in to 3in, or even wider, drawing attention to the waist. In February 1954, **Woman's Own** described the latest fashion in belts: 'Bicycle-clip belts are the latest thing in waist-huggers to give you a slender look. In different coloured leather or plastic, on a metal foundation, they are simply slipped round the waist. Priced at about 7/6d in plastic – more in leather.'

By August 1958, **Woman's Weekly** was reporting that: 'A new wide soft belt-cum-sash gives a new summer look for an old dress. A plain colour cotton dress will sparkle afresh given a sash-width belt of a two-tone cotton, with one colour to match the dress. A yellow frock gets a wide belt and deep buckle of yellow and white stripes.

'Or a pink dress is given a wide belt and buckle made from rose printed cotton. Get the buckle covered at a shop if it seems too difficult, but the belt is simply a double strip of fabric cut on the cross with the end neatened to a slant, jutting out for at least eight inches.'

The belt would remain an important part of women's wardrobes. Even in 1959, when the fashionable female shape had become more soft and rounded, belts continued to be worn with dresses.

## To Make Two, Two-colour Fair Isle Belts

_Materials for each belt:_
1 oz. in main colour and 1 oz. in contrast colour of 3-ply wool; a pair of No. 11 needles, 1 yard 1¼ins wide petersham or ribbon; 1 buckle.
_Measurements:_ width (finished) 1¾ins, length 36 ins.
_Tension:_ 8½ stitches and 10 rows to 1 in.

_Abbreviations:_ M.C. main colour, C.C. contrast colour.
**Striped belt:** with M.C. cast on 16 sts and work 4 rows in stocking-stitch.
Row 5 – (right side) knit 2 M.C., 12 C.C., 2 M.C.
Row 6 – purl as row 5.
Rows 7 to 10 – stocking-stitch using M.C.
Repeat rows 5 to 10 until belt measures 36 inches or length required. Cast off.
**Patterned belt:** With M.C. cast on 16 sts and work 2 rows in stocking-stitch.
Row 3 – (right side) Join in C.C., knit 2 M.C., 2 C.C., 8 M.C., 2 C.C., 2 M.C.
Row 4 – purl as row 3.
Row 5 – knit 4 M.C., 2 C.C., 4 M.C., 2 C.C., 4 M.C.
Row 6 – purl as row 5.
Row 7 – knit 6 M.C., 4 C.C., 6 M.C.
Row 8 – purl as row 7.
Rows 3 to 8 form the pattern, and are repeated until the belt measures 36 inches or length required. Cast off.
_To complete:_
Pin out and press under a damp cloth. Face knitting with petersham or ribbon and sew buckle to one end. Turn under the other end, if desired, to form a point and hem down on wrong side. Press again for a neat finish.

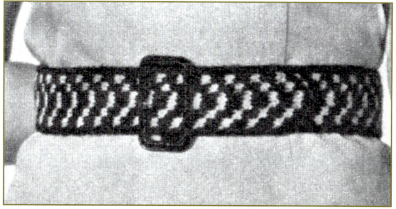

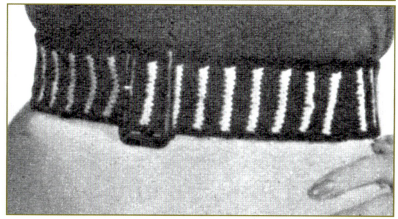

# Bags & Baskets

*No woman would dream of going out without her handbag. There were large bags for going shopping, smaller bags for day wear and elaborate bags for evenings out.*

▼ A selection of handbags, 1951.

**S**mooth soft leather handbags and elaborately styled shoes were a direct result of the Italian influence spread by such stars as Sophia Loren and Gina Lollobrigida. Bags came in all sorts of other materials, including raffia, wickerwork and the new soft plastics. Like everything else, the style was ostentatious, bright, with large fake fruit and flowers or heavy gilt chains.

### To Make a Beaded Evening Bag

*Materials:* One 4 oz. ball of No. 10 Macramé twine. A No. 10 crochet hook; an 8-inch matching zip fastener. 101 large beads in a contrast shade. Lining material.

*Measurements:* width of bag, 8 ins; depth 6 ins.

*Tension:* 6 d.c. and 8 rows measure 1 inch.

Make 51 ch. Fairly loosely, turn. Next row; Miss 1 ch., 50 d.c., in 50 ch. turn with 1 ch.

Next row: Miss 1 d.c., 49 d.c. in 49 d.c., turn with 1 ch. Repeat last row 4 times more. Break twine. Thread 99 beads on to the twine and with wrong side facing, work in beads as follows:

1st row: 4 d.c. in 4 d.c., * slip 1 bead close up to the hook, 5 d.c in 5 d.c.; repeat from * to end, turn with 1 ch..

2nd row: Miss 1 d.c., 49 d.c in 49 d.c., turn with 1 ch.

3rd row: 6 d.c. in 6 d.c., * slip 1 bead close up to hook, 5 d.c in 5 d.c.; repeat from * to last 3 d.c., slip 1 bead close up to hook, 3 d.c in 3 d.c., turn with 1 ch.

4th row: As 2nd.

5th row: As 1st.

6th – 12th rows: As 2nd.

13th – 17th rows: as 1st – 5th rows.

18th row: As 2nd.

19th row: As 3rd.

20th – 33rd rows: As 6th – 19th rows.

This completes the bead pattern and all 99 beads should be worked in.

Continue in plain d.c. until 100 rows have been done from start. Fasten off.

Press plain part on wrong side under a damp cloth. Cut lining material to fit bag, allowing $1/4$ inch all round for turnings. Fold lining in half, join short sides on wrong side. Tack a hem to wrong side all round top edge.

Fold crochet main part in half; join short sides. Stitch zip into opening very firmly with matching sewing cotton. Slip lining into bag and hem along top edge of zip; secure to lower corners of bag with a few stitches taken through the crochet.

Thread remaining two beads onto twine and crochet a chain 10 inches long, slipping a bead close up to hook $2^1/2$ inches from start and $2^1/2$ inches before end. Fasten off. Fold chain in four and knot through end of zip.

With increased leisure time, it became more important to have a suitable bag for your holiday; **Woman's Weekly**, July 1954, recommended that:

*'With your pretty outfits, a bag which is summery and light is almost a necessity. It can be a swing bag of tan leather or hide to go with tan shoes, or a bucket bag, or a home-made cotton drawstring to match a cotton dress. (Remember that this is not London, and black suede or leather will be out of place.)'*

# To Make a Bag for the Beach (1952)

Made of bright canvas, with bright, contrasting, binding around edge and hand-holes. Made in an hour or two from strong deck-chair canvas, or some similar fabric (plastic would be a good idea) to take your wet bathing things.

▲ A handmade beaded clutch bag, 1955. The beads meant it was probably for evening use.

*You need 2 oblongs, each 17 x 14 inches for back and front shapes; 2 oblongs, each 8 x 12 inches for lining handles; strip for gusset, 34 x 3 $1/2$ inches. By the yard, $3/4$ yard of 36-inch material, $1/2$ yard of 54-inch or $1^1/4$ yards of 26-inch; $5^1/2$ yards $1/2$-inch wide bias binding.*

Draw up your paper pattern and cut out; lay pattern on canvas and cut out back and front. Using top part of pattern only, cut out linings for back and front handles, i.e. these are exactly the same as back and front shapes but cut short just below opening. Cut lengths from remaining canvas to join together for gusset strip.

Lay linings inside back and front pieces and oversew outside edges together all round, then round inside of handles; leave bottom edges of lining loose inside bag and cover these edges with binding. Original binding was folded over the edge and stitched in position through all thicknesses in running stitches in thick cotton to match binding. Push a length of rolled braid, rug wool or thick cord up each handle to form a thickness round top; this makes the handles more comfortable to hold.

Bind each short end of gusset, then lay strip between back and front and oversew edges together all round; gusset ends come just above bottom of lining. Bind outside edges and inside handles as before.

Compacts, 1955.
Essential in every woman's handbag, compacts, 1959.
A range of handbags, 1955.

In 1955 Dior produced a huge white pigskin 'sausage bag' – a sort of cross between a large handbag and a long, unstiffened haversack or small hammock – while Roger Model produced, among others, a suede bag, *'shaped like a child's schoolbag'*. As fashionable shapes changed, bags made from expensive materials could not just be dumped. In **Vogue**, July 1955, there were several adverts offering to repair and renovate your bag, including: *'Broken frames repaired, new frames fitted, new zips fitted'* or *'Your crocodile handbag repaired and relined to a modern style and renovated as new from 60/-'* and *'Any crocodile, snake and leather bags remodelled.'*

As with everything else, the new plastics were used extensively for cheap, yet bright and fashionable bags; towards the end of the decade even perspex bags appeared.

Straw was popular for baskets, often decorated with bright raffia flowers, giving them a Mediterranean feel. **Woman's Weekly** gave advice on how to clean a straw basket: *'Water will not harm the straw of your basket. I suggest that you brush the straw thoroughly, to remove any excess dust, then, to half a pint of tepid water add the juice of half a lemon. Dip the brush in the lemon water from time to time, but avoid making the basket too wet. Work methodically so that the whole basket is cleaned. Then when you have covered the complete surface, wring out a piece of clean muslin in fresh, tepid water and wipe all over the basket. If possible, leave it to dry out of doors.'*

# Cases

*Increasing spare time and wages meant more holidays, and the need for good luggage grew with them.*

**Foreign** travel was a luxury in the early 1950s, and as such was to be aspired to. An element of such travel was cases, preferably matching and of modern styling. You might not be able to afford the continental holiday, but you could perhaps afford the luggage and if nothing else, a vanity case. At Christmas 1955 one advert in **Men Only** ran: *'Your present problems are a thing of the past when you buy her a Vanity Case like this one by Noton. Beautifully fitted with polythene bottles and jars, it costs about 75/-.'*

As the decade went on, and wages rose, holiday travel increased, and trips abroad became more and more accessible to ordinary people. Good luggage became important – you did not want to arrive at your hotel with the cardboard suitcase given to Dad on his demob – and good-looking cases in modern designs sold well.

umbrellas became

▲ A selection of women's cases.

▶ Modern matching suitcases gave an air of class.

# Umbrellas

*Man-made fibres such as nylon meant that umbrellas could be both waterproof and lightweight – excellent for the sophisticated look the fifties demanded.*

**Women's** sophisticated – long and thin were the operative words – and brightly coloured, both in the material and the handle, which might be candy-striped. The use of man-made materials for both the handle and the canopy meant that they could be light and showerproof. When not in use, the material could be tightly furled, making it very slender and elegant.

The French company Vedrenne sold umbrellas that unscrewed in the middle, so that handles could be easily changed, thus creating several umbrellas.

With the fashion for Chinese-style clothes in the late 1950s, the traditional lacquered paper parasol made a comeback.

The umbrella was also very much part of the Edwardian-revival look favoured by some men in the mid-1950s. However, the habitual carrying of an umbrella started to be seen as somewhat stuffy and old-fashioned, and it became increasingly a wet-weather necessity rather than a fashion accessory.

# Spectacles

*'The day of round, owl-like spectacles has gone for ever. Today the accent is on style, colour, shape of lens. So don't be timid: invest an extra guinea or so in a "new look" and cut a dash', **Everywoman**, June 1955.*

## glasses

. . . choose frames that flatter good features, tone down bad, add piquancy to colour schemes

◄ **Change-abouts** . . . *frames with slots into which you slip brows to suit mood or colour schemes. Bateman*

**Sunlovers ►** . . . *up-to-the-minute frames to take your ordinary pre-scription. Note sinuous sides. Stanley Unger*

*Newest of all, panoramic frame gives uninterrupted vision at the sides with curved lenses.* Stanley Unger

*Motif on a sinuous-sided frame calls attention to a fine complexion and softens that hard side view.* Melson Wingate

Spectacles stayed very much the same in the immediate post-war years: basically round for men, in black or brown plastic, or wire with a plastic cover, and similar, but sometimes slightly more oval, for women and children. Uncovered wire frames, usually a sort of rounded square shape and often with a quiet pattern worked into the metal, were also available for both men and women, the latter also having the choice of tiny brilliants set in for evening wear.

However, on the whole the British public in the early 1950s was rather conservative about its glasses. **Woman's Own**, October 1953, pointed out that: *'Once an American takes to glasses, he makes them part of his dress and charac-ter, and he picks them as carefully as his suits. The Frenchman prefers dignified frames. The Briton? He just does not care; when he wears glasses he's thoroughly untidy. The latest styles in frames are the same in all three countries – so the Briton has only himself to blame!'*

By the date of the letter, the classic 1950s shape frame was beginning to appear: the winged top, known as cat's

eyes, or perhaps more racily, devil's eyes. These evolved slowly, becoming more point-ed, narrower and exaggerated. **Woman's Weekly**, July 1954, advised: *'Look for spectacles with a narrow bridge (perhaps a thin metal one) and frames in which the upper rims curve upwards away from the bridge. The optician might be able to arrange for the bridge to come a fraction further down your nose than is usual, to give the effect of shortening it. Most opticians are realising the cosmetic value of spectacles nowadays and are only too willing to co-operate in the choosing of flattering ones.'*

Have a look at the fastest spreading **RUMOR** in town

KARAT TOP METAKON

ALUKON

AND *Thunderbird* TRADEMARK

Des. Patent Pending on Frame

**Kono**

▲ Some very striking glasses and sunglasses, 1955.
◄◄ Glasses are slowly moving away from the traditional round shape, 1952.
◄ By 1959, the arms had become very heavy, as is seen in the lower two pairs of spectacles.
▼ Classic 'cat's eyes', 1957.

**Ti-To** *The Timely Frame offers you a sound solution to your trim problem!*

▶ Jewelled glasses bacme fashionable for evening wear.

▶ By 1955, the classic 1950s look had evolved.

▶▼ By 1953 the 'brows' of the glasses are beginning to take on the classic 'cat's eyes' shape.

▼ 'Cat's eyes' glasses became one of the icons of the 1950s.

**Everywoman,** June 1955, advised that: *'Your optician will guide you in the choice of a frame. You will have a straight "brow" or slanting, according to the tilt of your eyebrows; high bridge or low, according to the shape of your nose; narrow or wide frames according to the shape of your face. But you can choose the colour – even buy frames with brows that slot in and out to change with your mood (but be wary of red – it must match lipstick exactly). Choose too, between glass and plastic lenses. The latter won't break, are lightweight and ideal for sport, can cost a trifle more than glass.*

*'Watch too, for sinuous sided frames that soften the profile; motifs to draw attention to a flawless complexion and a pretty ear; panoramic lenses that curve "round the corner" to give uninterrupted vision; sunglasses that are more adventurous than ever (if you can't afford a separate pair, have your everyday lenses faintly tinted when buying those new frames).'*

The article mentions frames with brows that slot in and out; these were designed to be several pairs in one: a single pair of glasses (thus saving cost) but with interchangeable 'wings' in different colours or styles: fairly plain for work, decorated and jewelled for going out. There was also the option of bi-focal and tri-focal lenses (an early version of the varifocal).

For men, the shape evolved from the circle to the square, via a sort of round-cornered square. Heavy plastic frames became widespread, but you could still get wire frames, although these were not popular.

As the decade wore on the fashion was for the arms of the frames to become heavier and

FOR CLASSIC BEAUTY

*Motif*

DESIGNED BY ZYLITE

No. W404/3
*Ebony on White*

No. P402/3    No. W402/3
*Pink*            *White*

No. W412/3
*Silver & Black on White*

No. P414/3
*Charcoal & Bronze on Pink*

more shaped. Women could choose from a wide range of colours and finishes: engraved, inlaid with mother-of-pearl or contrasting coloured plastic, or adorned with small plastic shapes such as flowers or birds, or marcasite: *'Lovely eyes with tilted outer corners are enhanced by glittering glasses'*, **London Life**, May 1958. Men tended to stick with black, although brown and two-tone were available, as well as a sort of horizontally striped plastic that had a wood effect, and while these were popular in the USA they were less so in Britain.

In the last few years of the 1950s the trend was for the arms and brows to remain thick plastic, but for the bottom of the frame to be in wire. Cat's eye shapes diminished in popularity, although of course some women continued to wear them, and a gentler, rounded square returned.

▲ A series of women's frames, 1959.

▲▲ A mixture of plastic and metal frames, 1953. These would become very fashionable by the end of the decade.

▲▲▲ Advert for combined spectacles/hearing aid, 1953.

# Sunglasses

In July 1952, the noted artist Sir William Russell Flint wrote a letter to **The Times** in which he complained bitterly about young women who wore: *'strangely shaped and curiously tinted spectacles, and think them just the thing'*. He thought they thereby: *'not only hide but weaken their illustrious orbs, reduce their chances of conquest, and cause deprivation to the male population'*. Needless to say there was quite a flood of letters rebutting his ideas.

Sunglasses not only fitted in with the emphasis on leisure fashions, and the desire to appear part of the foreign-holiday smart set, they were also worn by famous film stars and music stars seeking (not always very hard) to avoid photographers, again adding to their desirability as a fashion accessory. This was added to once again as Italian fashions hit the scene, with photographs of sophisticated men in sharp suits and, of course, sunglasses.

There were, as Sir William had noted, many shapes and tints of sunglasses on the market, from the very cheap plastic, all-in-one-piece glasses through to the clip-ons – *The Sol sun shield fits over your own glasses – automatically fits any frame in 2 seconds a wrap around sheet of plastic – cost 2/3d'*, advert from July 1952 – to expensive polaroids and Ray-Bans. Many frames followed the fashionable shapes in spectacles, only more so, and then as now, people became far more daring on holiday – in 1955 Patou sold *'Devil's eye sunglasses linked by a coloured plastic chain'*.

▲ Sunglasses for the whole family, 1957.
▶ Polaroid advert, 1953.

## ONLY *POLAROID* sunglasses eliminate glare!

Unlike ordinary sunglasses which darken everything you see, Polaroid Sunglasses with their selective control over light, enable you to see through reflected glare yet retain clear detail and sparkling colour in everything you wish to see. Ideal for Holidays, Motoring, Angling, Boating, etc.

*as seen with the naked eye..*

*...with ordinary sun glasses*

-Now *see* how only

★ **POLAROID**

sunglasses – **absorb** harmful glare! **guard** the eyes!

YOUR PROTECTION — Ask to see the Polaroid Test before buying

OBTAINABLE FROM OPTICIANS, CHEMISTS, SPORTS DEALERS, AND DEPARTMENTAL STORES EVERYWHERE

# Jewellery

*Yet another casualty of the war, jewellery came back with a bang in the 1950s, generally the more ostentatious the better.*

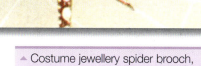

The fashion for chunky jewellery extended to necklaces, bracelets, earrings, rings and brooches. Boldness was not limited to size – opulence was the word. If you could afford it, large gold jewellery, or pearls, or a diamond bracelet were just the thing. For the rest, chunky gilt metal, diamante, plastic pearls and heavy costume jewellery was the answer – the bigger the better. This was the rule for buttons, too, crystal, gilt and paste being favourites, with buttons on dresses and coats often being large.

In 1953 the millions who watched the Coronation saw a feast of jewels – tiaras, necklaces, etc. – and this influenced popular fashion, with glittering costume jewellery splashed over evening wear. For day wear the main items remained earrings, especially the single pearl type. This shape continued to be popular, although now bigger than had been the case – about the size of a modern 10 pence piece. Women's magazines suggested making your own earrings from a pair of old gilt or crystal buttons stuck on earring backs. Pendant earrings were also popular, such as drop-pearl earrings or gypsy hoops. The other common piece of day jewellery was the necklace, most commonly a close-fitting single, double or triple string of pearls or beads.

In May 1954, **Woman's Weekly** informed its readers that: *'Each summer there is one special fashion for neckwear in the way of jewellery. This year it is the mass of white beads. Find, beg, or borrow every strand you can, whatever their size. Put them all together in what appears to be a tangled mass. The effect will be stunningly smart.'* In July the magazine advised its readers to: *'choose very carefully a few costume ornaments such as earrings, a necklet and bracelet. If you keep them all to say, gilt in winter and white beads in summer, you will never look wrongly trimmed.'*

▲ Costume jewellery spider brooch, 1955.
◀ A tight pearl necklace and a pearl earring, always acceptable for day wear.
▼ Ciro Pearls advert, 1956. The single or multiple string of pearls remained fashionable throughout the 1950s.

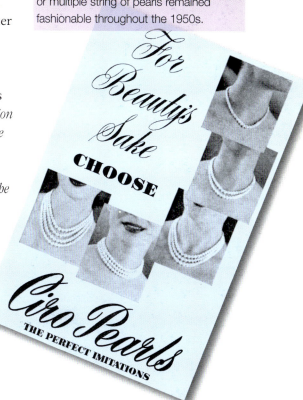

For Beauty's Sake CHOOSE Ciro Pearls
THE PERFECT IMITATIONS

# To Make a Pin-up Necklace and Matching Bracelet (1954)

'To make necklace, you need 60 small safety pins and 32 large ones, 25, ⅝in. diameter curtain rings, and 24 inches of narrow ribbon.

'Working from curtain ring as centre, slip on to it 16 large safety pins (heads facing centre). Dividing these into groups of four, slip each group through four more curtain rings; so that either side of the centre you have a double row. Then link another four large pins to each ring; to the next ring link four small pins, and so on, gradually decreasing number of pins. Excluding central ring, there should be an upper and lower row of 12 rings each. For tie fastening, stitch two 12-in. pieces of ribbon into last rings.

'For matching bracelet, take 16 large safely pins and 28 small ones, 1 yard narrow black ribbon, and 12 ⅝in. diameter curtain rings. Place two rings opposite each other, and working from these link on to each 6 small pins. Divide into groups of three, slip pin-ends of each group through a curtain ring. Link up into circle, using following numbers of pins for each join: 4 small, 4 large, 4 large, 4 small, 3 small. Stitch small piece ribbon to last ring. Make ribbon bow, fasten to other end ring. Attach half press stud each side for fastening.'

The fashion in 1955 was for as many strings of beads as possible to be worn on the wrist as bracelets, or alternatively, groups of plastic Indian bangles might be worn, several on each wrist; the number is indicated by the fact that they were sold by the dozen (10/-), as were the matching finger rings (3/-). Also worn in groups were the very latest in necklaces. These were long – waist length, like those of the flappers In the 1920s – and were often worn with twin-set and trousers.

Daytime earrings were fairly large, but plain, while for evening wear the fashion was for very large imitation (genuine if you could afford it) gemstone earrings, brooches, bracelets and necklaces. Once again, three or four bracelets would be worn together. The Dior Boutique in Paris sold oval turquoise and rhinestone earrings (turquoise blue was the colour in Paris that year) and a four-stringed bracelet with each string made up of alternate big blue beads and pearls.

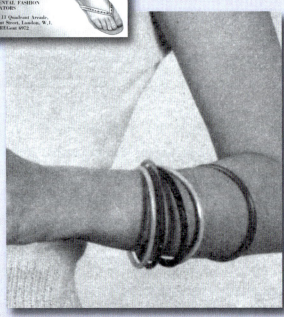

◀ Indian-look bangles and rings, 1955.
▼ A collection of bangles, the height of fashion in the mid-1950s.

## To Make a Bead Necklace (1955)

'A smart necklace of black and white beads with little pearls in between is the latest fashion and can be made very easily. If you wear it twisted three or four times round the throat it will fill in the neckline of a summer frock most attractively. Or it will look equally pretty as a bracelet wound many times round your wrist. You will need the following: one hundred and four white beads (These are sold for putting around milk-jug covers). A black bead necklace of 43 beads which you can find in the multiple stores for about 1/6d. Nylon thread with clasp attached. And a packet of 290 embroidery pearls or glass beads.

'The beads should be threaded in the following order. Clasp, 2 white beads, * 2 pearls, 1 black bead, 2 pearls, 1 white bead, 2 pearls, 1 white bead, repeat from * to the end of the necklace, then attach 2 white beads and then the other half of the clasp.'

By 1956 simplicity was back, with the short, single string of pearls being the fashion. Less common would be a double string or a string of single coloured beads, amber if you could afford them, otherwise plastic. Earrings, too, were small and fairly plain.

By 1958, the fashionable idea was most definitely that big was beautiful. **London Life** that May declared: 'Jewels must be chunky to be smart', and advised its readers to 'wear a glittering three-inch wide bracelet, allied to a huge ring and pink-pearl nail polish. . . . bunchy earrings of various coloured sea pearls are a smart touch. . . . or a heavy charm bracelet and huge star ring.'

1959 saw long strings of beads, either worn flapper style, or wound four or five times round the neck. Women's hair was now worn fairly short, but often covered the ears, so earrings were not always worn. When they were worn, they would commonly be large pearls or paste clusters or dangly paste pendants. With them might be worn a couple of simple bangles or a single, chunky bracelet.

◄ Chunky costume jewellery was the thing for evening wear.
▼ Ciro plastic and marcasite brooches and matching earrings, 1959.
▼▼ Engagement rings, 1953.

DIAMONDS SET IN PLATINUM AND 18 ct.

For men, jewellery was rarer than ever and generally comprised the gold or silver signet ring, wedding band and cuff-links – tie pins were still seen, but far more rarely as the wide ties of the late 1940s and early '50s looked silly with them. Regimental badges were popular in cuff-links, as were car badges and fox-hunting scenes. **Men Only**, December 1955, reported that: *'Among the nicest things I've seen for the male Christmas tree this year is a pair of gold cuff-links with foxes' heads and minute rubies for the eyes, or a similar pair with small running foxes but sans rubies. Others showed dogs, horses, and some, cars.'*

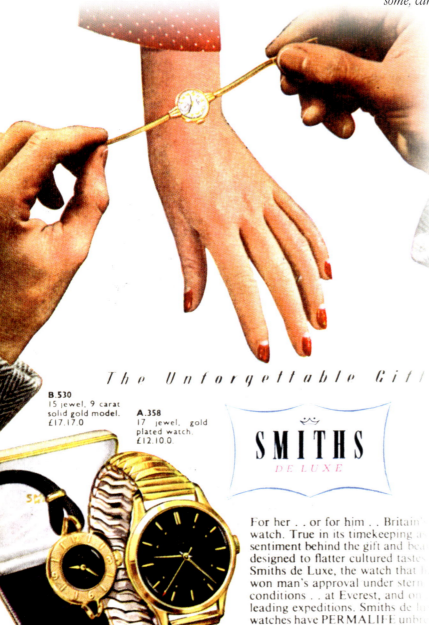

*The Unforgettable Gift*

**B.530**
15 jewel, 9 carat solid gold model.
£17.17.0

**A.358**
17 jewel, gold plated watch.
£12.10.0

# SMITHS
## DE LUXE

For her . . or for him . . Britain's watch. True in its timekeeping sentiment behind the gift and be designed to flatter cultured taste Smiths de Luxe, the watch that won man's approval under stern conditions . . at Everest, and on leading expeditions. Smiths de watches have PERMALIFE unbr mainsprings and the movements unconditionally guaranteed for one Sold exclusively by Jewellers from £8.19.6 to £63.0.0.

## Watches

Men's watches became plainer, almost universally round and thinner and platinum plated models became fashionable. Calendar dials – *'Automatic action changes date every 24 hours'* – were still unusual. Expanding bracelets became more common, although the leather strap remained the norm. Pocket watches, and watch chains, previously worn with waistcoats, disappeared with the waistcoat. They hung on for a while with the dinner suit as the stiff cuff made a wrist watch impractical, but, as **Men Only** magazine, December 1955, reported: *'since the dinner-suit shirt has gone soft-cuffed, there's nothing whatever against wearing a wrist-watch.'* Women's watches, like men's, were round, although fancy, jewelled evening watches or jewelled evening-wear pendant watches were still produced.

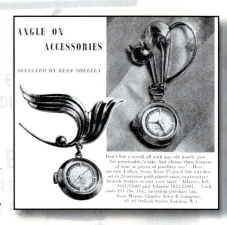

**ANGLE ON ACCESSORIES**
*SELECTED BY ELSA SHELLEY*

Don't fob yourself off with any old watch, just for punctuality's sake, but choose these keepers of time as pieces of jewellery too! Here are two Loftus, Swiss lever 17-jewel fob watches, set in 20 microns gold-plated cases, in attractive brooch designs to suit your taste – Atlantic, left, 1622/11060 and Atlantic 1623/11061. Each costs £11 19s. 11d., including purchase tax, from Messrs. Charles Astor & Company, 81-83 Oxford Street, London, W.1.

◄ Men's and women's watches, 1955.
▲ Ladies' pendant watches, 1956.
▼ Classic men's watch, 1953.

STAINLESS STEEL.

# Scarves, Stoles & Capes

*'A scarf made from a print square, tied round the neck in a loose, casual knot is another variation of the print fashion. The scarf should match your belt', **Woman's Weekly**, August 1958.*

**Stoles** made from fur or brightly coloured fabrics were worn at all times of the day, and in many different ways. **Stitchcraft** magazine, June 1952, advised: *'As a change from the ever-lasting headsquare, buy a yard of rayon or silk (silk is best if you can afford it as it is less slippery) – cut it in half length-ways, join the short ends neatly, slip-hem long raw edges, and you have a manoeuvrable long stole which can be worn in all sorts of ways and is so much prettier and smarter than a triangle tied under your chin. Carry it around on holiday and it will be a godsend for those chilly moments and less bother to carry than a cardigan. Worn round your neck, with the ends tied at the back under your arms it makes a snug bolero. As a cardigan – round your shoulders then the ends taken under your belt, up and under your belt again in two comfortable pockets. Worn as a stole around the shoulders or over the head with the ends crossed in front and taken back over the shoulders. Tie it around your waist when you don't want to carry it.'*

## To Knit a Feather-light Stole for Late-day Occasions

Size: 66 ins. by 22 ins. (without fringe).

Materials: 5 oz. 2 ply wool. 1 pair each of No. 7 and No. 9 knitting needles.

Tension: 7 sts to 1 in.

The pattern is a multiple of 18 sts plus 3 edge sts at each end of the rows. Cast on 18 sts more for a wider stole, or 18 sts fewer for a narrower one.

Using No. 7 needles, cast on 2 sts., * insert needle between last 2 sts and k. 1, place loop on left-hand needle; rep. from * until there are 150 sts. K. 1 row, then change to No. 9 needles and work in following patt:

1st row. – K. 3, * sl. 1, k. 1, pass slipped stitch over (wool forward, k. 2 tog.), 3 times, wool forward, k. 2 (wool forward, k. 2 tog.), 4 times; rep. from * to last 3 sts, k. 3.

2nd row. – K.

3rd row. – K. 3, * sl. 1, k. 1, pass slipped stitch over, k. 6, wool forward, k. 2, wool forward, k. 6, k. 2 tog.; rep from * to last 3 sts, k. 3.

4th row. – K. 3, then p. to last 3 sts, k. 3.

5th row. – as 3rd row.

6th row. – K.

These 6 rows form the pattern. Continue to work thus until 4½ oz. of wool have been used, or for length required, ending with first pattern row. Change to No. 7 needles, k. 1 row. Cast off loosely.

Fringe. – *Wind 10 strands of wool round a 6 in. wide book. Slip loops off the book, then pass the double loops through eyelet hole for ½ in., then pass the other end of loops through and form a knot. Rep. from * into every alternate eyelet at both ends of the stole, then cut through the loops.

## To Make a Double-sided Cape (1953)

Velvet side out, wear it for parties and the theatre. The pixie ear pieces and snug under-the-chin tie will keep you warm on chilly evenings and the velvet lends a lovely richness to any outfit. Turned inside out, the cape has a new character. The gay check fabric brightens any top coat on a windy day and keeps you warm on shopping tours, or on country walks.

Materials; ¾ yd of velvet and ¾ yd of checked woollen material. Make a pattern from the diagram – each square represents 2 square inches. Allow half an inch all round for turnings.

Fold velvet in half and lay pattern as shown. Cut out two pieces. Sew up darts, then sew pieces together along back seam. Repeat with woollen material, making sure your checks align. Sew up darts and back seam. Place velvet and wool together, wrong side out, and machine two sides together. Turn right inside out and hemstitch third side. Make two velvet ribbons and sew to front of hood.

## An Easy-to-make 'Pocket Stole' designed by Norman Hartnell (1959)

Make your stole in white pique or poplin to wear over pretty summer dresses . . . and for holidays it can be made in towelling to wear on the beach.

This attractive stole has flap pockets and is shaped by small pleats at the centre back so that it fits cleverly round the shoulders. The stole is cut double with a centre back seam which is concealed by a buttoned band.

available in most of the authentic Scottish tartans – highly desirable if you've got Scots ancestry

FRONT

FOLD

BACK SEAM

# Men

Scarves altered little, although the materials changed a lot. As with just about everything else, by the mid-1950s, synthetic, or synthetic mixes, were all the rage, although cashmere was even better if you could afford it. **Men Only**, December 1955, recommended as a present a *'new scarf made of 70% pure cashmere, 30% fine wool, which is now available in men's or women's styles. It's available in most of the authentic Scottish tartans – highly desirable whether you've got Scots ancestry or whether you just like tartans – 31/6d.'*

Another new scarf material was a: *'plain wool muffler scarf'* – a kind of fine tweed. Some men found these a problem to wear, as described by one reader of **Men Only**: *'If one just wraps it over, without a knot, it doesn't do its job; if one knots it, it seems altogether too bulky; and either way, it doesn't look neat enough. What's the secret?'* Once again, **Men Only** supplied the answer: *'With the scarf at full length, fold the two long edges under, to meet down the centre. Then tie this narrowed scarf round the neck, using a single knot in front. Arrange so that the front end covers the back and centrally (as in an ordinary necktie) and then unfold the front part only, to fill the neck opening neatly.'*

## To Knit a Man's Scarf (1953)

Materials: three ounces of 3-ply fingering, a set of 4 No. 12 knitting needles pointed at both ends, a pair of No. 10 needles, a No. 9 crochet hook.

Tension and measurements: Worked at such a tension that two repeats of the pattern (20 sts.) measure 2¼ inches in width with No. 10 needles. After light pressing the scarf will measure 6¼ inches wide and 42 inches long.

To work: With No. 10 needles cast on 60 sts and work in pattern as follows:

1st Row: All p.
2nd Row: (K. 9, p. 1) 6 times.
3rd Row: (K. 2, p. 8) 6 times.
4th Row: (K. 7, p. 3) 6 times.
5th Row: (K. 4, p. 6) 6 times.
6th Row: (K. 5, p. 5) 6 times.
7th Row: (K. 6, p. 4) 6 times.
8th Row: (K. 3, p. 7) 6 times.
9th Row: (K. 8, p. 2) 6 times.
10th Row: (K. 1, p. 9) 6 times.
11th Row: All k.

Work back from the 10th to 2nd row inclusive.

These 20 rows form the pattern. Repeat them 19 times more. Cast off straight across.

With right side of work facing, and using No. 9 crochet hook, work a row of d.c. all round the scarf, working into each st. of the row ends at the sides, and each st. of the cast-on and cast-off edges.

Press lightly with a hot iron over a damp cloth.

To Make the Fringe: Cut 5 strands of wool each 7 inches long, and fold them at the centre so that all the ends meet. Take a crochet hook and insert this through the first d.c. along the edge of scarf. Draw the looped end of the short strands through the hole, then with the fingers draw all the cut ends of the wool through the looped end, then draw up closely with a sharp downward pull.

Repeat this in every alternate d.c. along both ends of the scarf. How to Work Double Crochet: Begin by putting the crochet hook through one stitch on the edge and draw the wool through to make a loop, * insert hook into the next stitch and draw wool through two loops now on hook. Wool over hook and draw through both loops, when there will be one loop left on hook, continue from * to end.

# Hairstyles

*'Every now and then take yourself off to a really good hairdresser and have a permanent wave and slightly different hair style. This is even more of an uplift than a new hat', Woman's Weekly, July 1952.*

In the 1950s it was usual to wash and style your hair at home, but chemical permanent waving solutions were sufficiently dangerous and unpredictable to send most women to the increasing band of professional hairdressers. Typically, hair would be cut and permed every six or seven weeks, and once a week, or once a fortnight if money was a bit short, hair would be washed and set, again by the hairdresser. **Everywoman**, June 1955, wrote: *'Today there are 34,000 hairdressing salons in Great Britain, and 110,000 staff. Sixty per cent of women have their hair permed regularly – the average woman spends twenty hours a year in a salon and pays out £8 a year; in Rene's Mayfair women spend about £5 a week!'*

Even schoolgirls slept in wire and coin rollers, kept in place by hairnets or silk scarves. The Lady Jayne slumber helmet was said to: *'preserve the most expensive hairdo throughout each night, saving money on hair dressing and time in the morning. In pastel nets and laces.'*

There was still a widespread belief that washing your hair frequently would damage it. **Woman's Weekly**, March 1959, advised that: *'You should wash your hair as soon as you feel it needs it. Some hair becomes lank and greasy very quickly but, if you keep it very short, it isn't so much trouble to wash and dry it very quickly.'* **Woman's Own**, February 1954, discussed the problem: *'To give new life to lank hair, supplement your shampoos with in-between brushing, using shredded cotton strips between the brush bristles. Remove and renew the strips as they become soiled.'*

Of course, washing your hair could actually be dangerous in a time when central heating and double-glazing were rarities, as one **Woman's Companion** reader pointed out: *'I don't have a hair dryer, and unless I can be sure of staying in the warm until my hair is quite dry, I quickly catch cold. I often used to use a dry shampoo in winter, but I find these difficult to obtain now.'* The magazine responded that: *'Powdered orris root, obtainable from chemists, is an excellent substitute for dry shampoo and is used in just the same way. Put it into a talcum powder dispenser, puff it over your hair, leave for about twenty minutes, then brush out thoroughly with a scrupulously clean brush. This removes all grease and leaves the hair soft and fluffy.'*

▸ Amami advert, 1949. The long free hair styles of the late 1940s would soon be replaced by more tightly permed shorter hair.

▴ Perming and setting required rollers, with many women sleeping in rollers such as these every night.

## Waves & Curls

*make your hair alluring*

Whatever the style of your set it will look most lovely and *stay lovely all day* if you use quick-drying non-sticky, Amami Wave Set. If your hair is of normal texture use Amami GREEN Wave Set. If it is fine and easy-to-manage use Amami SPIRITOUS Wave Set. 1/1½d. and 2/6½d.
Ask for AMAMI *and see that you get it.*

## AMAMI
### WAVE SET

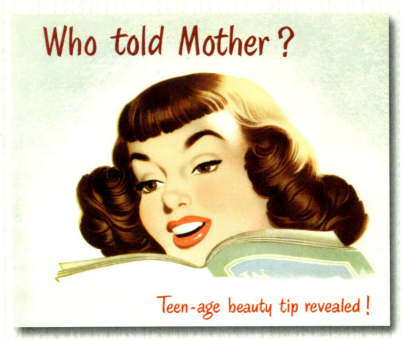

Who told Mother?

Teen-age beauty tip revealed!

**Woman's Weekly**, March 1959, advised that: *'You will also find hair lacquer is a useful beauty aid. When you haven't time for a shampoo, simply spray on the lacquer and pin or brush your hair into shape. It will immediately gain new crispness and look tidy again until you can manage to wash it. An excellent quick-drying lacquer is available for 1/6d.'* Castor oil applied warm to hair a few hours before shampooing was said to give *'a lovely natural sheen'* to hair after it had been washed, though hair had to be washed extremely thoroughly to remove all the oil.

Colouring hair was popular. Peroxide blondes had been around since long before the war, but there were side effects of such

harsh treatments. **Woman's Weekly**, March 1952, warned: *'Drop the idea of bleaching your hair with peroxide. If used regularly it softens the structure of the hair and dries up the natural oils. The hair starts breaking and splitting and there will come a time when it won't take a permanent wave.'*

The answer for many was a colour rinse. The **Academy of Charm and Beauty** gave instructions for using these: *'Hair cosmetics have made great strides recently, especially in the field of colour rinses. A rinse is not a dye. It washes out at each shampooing. When used properly it brings out highlights and adds lustre as well as a little colour.*

*'It is . . . much better and wiser to leave the application of tints and dyes to a skilled hairdresser. But if you do decide to treat your hair at home, to get the best results from your rinse you must, of course, first shampoo your hair thoroughly . . . and then rinse thoroughly with water. This last water rinse is very important, for it must remove all soap so that no film is left on the hair.*

*'Then apply the colour rinse, preferably with a small brush. Part your hair down the centre of the head, then dip the brush in the rinse solution and brush it up from the roots halfway to the ends of your hair. (Hair ends are usually porous and take on the colour faster than the rest of the hair, so in order to keep the rinse application even leave the ends till last). Part the hair again about one-quarter of an inch from the first part and repeat the process until you*

have covered your whole head. Then run your comb through your hair down to the ends. Dilute the unused portion of the rinse with water and pour it on your hair. Leave it on for a few minutes, then rinse with clear water. Apply a cream hair dressing for that final shiny, well-groomed look.'

For many women rinses were used to cover grey hair, or the appearance of a few grey hairs. **Everywoman**, June 1955, recommended that: 'On grey hair use an ash or steel grey rinse, on pure white use a golden one.' Alternatively, **Woman's Weekly**, August 1958, suggested that: 'You may like to choose a colour slightly lighter than your own dark hair – then the grey hairs will gleam with a copper light which could be very attractive. This type of rinse will wash out again if you do not like the effect. If you find it successful, you might try one of the cream hair colourings which last through about six shampoos and so save yourself the trouble of a rinse each time you wash your hair. If the grey hairs are all in one spot you can dramatise them with a silver hair cosmetic, making a fascinating streak in the front, or wings at the side. These cosmetics are sprayed, puffed or painted on and can be removed by brushing or washing.' The **Academy of Charm and Beauty** was more specific: 'If you're 10–20 per cent grey you should choose a colour three shades lighter than your own hair. This will blend in with the grey hair, but won't add too much colour to your original hair shade. Adding more colour to the part that isn't grey would make your hair too dark. If your hair is 20–50 per cent grey choose a colour two shades lighter – because you have more grey hair to colour, less that will turn darker. For hair over 50 per cent grey, choose a colour to match your own hair. Apply tint to greyest portion first.'

Tints and rinses were certainly

not only for grey hair. Camilatone, one of the more popular makes of colour rinse, came in honey gold, blonde rose, auburn, amber, chestnut, dark brown, raven black, blue (silver white) and golden rinse. **Everywoman**, June 1955, suggested that:

'If you have a rinse, you can choose the colour to go with your eyes, or your make-up, or your clothes. But a permanent tint or bleach must be matched absolutely to the skin or it looks ugly and artificial. It is best to go back to your natural colour, or a slightly more vivid version of it. If you want to bleach dark hair, make the final colour a tawny amber that often, in fact, accompanies a dark complexion. Use a golden rinse for a darkened blonde, a silvery one on dark ash hair, chestnut on mid-brown hair, and titian on dark hair.'

There were a number of alternatives to rinses. **Woman's Companion**, October 1958, listed: 'Brighteners, rinses, semi-permanent tints, tips and streaks for the hair are becoming more and more popular, and I've seen many marvellous transformations. A bright rinse can make all the difference to a simple practical cut. And in artificial light a concentrated splash of colour is the final touch to an evening hair style.' **Woman's Own**, February 1954, recommended: 'A streak of lightening goes to your hair in the way of a new quick-to-apply cosmetic, with a shimmering effect. Designed to give you a contrast streak or highlight your curls, it is by hairstylist French of London. It comes in Quicksilver, Demon Gold, Tiger Bronze and is applied with a brush – price 7s 6d.' **Woman's Companion**, December 1958, advised: 'For something special, you could streak sections of your hair with

The only setting lotion made to suit *your* hair texture

**Amami** *Wave Set*

Only Amami Wave Set is made to suit differing hair textures. That's why it's *always* successful. That's why your 'set' takes more easily, looks lovelier—and lasts so much longer when you use Amami. Easy to use, quick to set, it coaxes every type of hair into soft, shining waves and curls. Get Amami today!

**GREEN** for hair that can be difficult.

**SPIRIT** for easier-to-manage hair.

*Handy flacks* 1/4½ *Large economy size* 2/7½

*N.B.* MORE WOMEN USE AMAMI WAVE SET THAN ALL OTHER SETTING LOTIONS PUT TOGETHER

▼ Hair style from 1954. A freer, younger, less tightly controlled style was evolving.

*gold or silver. To do this, make a small hole in a piece of paper or cardboard, then take a few strands of hair and pull through. Now spray the strand with gold or silver dust, or you could use one of the latest highlighting preparations that come in lipstick form.'*

The permanent wave remained the basis of the hairstyle for the majority of women. Home perm outfits were available, as described by **Woman's Companion**, November 1958: *'If you do your own perming at home . . . you can choose an outfit planned and prepared to give a really soft, casual wave. I think you would be very interested in the newest lanolised pin curl perm created specially for home use. These pin curl perms are very kind to the hair and, according to your individual hair type, will last from six to twelve weeks. The difference with this method is that there's no fuss with end papers, no unwinding, no resetting. From the time you wind up your curls,* *fixing them with pins or grips, until the time you comb out your dry hair, soft, curly and beautifully set, it is never unpinned.'* But for most women, if they could afford it, a visit to the hairdresser was far preferable.

When permanent waving first became popular in the pre-war period most women had two perms a year, usually strong and very tightly wound. Often the result was a sort of frizz for the first two or three months while it settled down, while the second three months were usually happier ones with nicely curly, easily manageable hair. By the 1950s most women had learnt that it was more sensible to have three light perms a year rather than two strong ones, giving far better results from the start. With the much more frequent trimming demanded by the hairstyles then in vogue, the perm was usually almost all out after three to four months.

It was most important that your perm was allowed to grow out fully: *'Probably your hair seems straight to you because it won't hold a set until the next washing time, but if you examine it very carefully when it is wet at shampoo time you will be able to see for certain whether your hair is without perm or whether there is just the slightest "kink" left from the last one. If there is, then another perm on top of it would most certainly cause frizz'*, **Woman's Companion**, November 1958.

Even so there were still disasters – the perm that instead of being soft waves and pretty curls was just a mass of frizz being the most usual. A perm had to be prepared for, and the **Academy of Charm and Beauty** gave assistance on this: *'We all know that the condition of your hair has a great deal to do with the success or failure of your new permanent wave. So about a month before your date with the hairdresser, work at putting your hair into tip-top condition and health. Keep your hair especially clean during this period. Shampoo weekly – two sudsings each time. For stimulation and more thorough cleansing use a small brush.'* A reader of **Woman's Weekly** wrote, August 1952: *'Since my last permanent wave my hair has got noticeably thinner and lost its natural sheen which worries me.'* The reply was:

'It sounds as if your hair was not in very good condition when you had it permanently waved. Your best plan would be to give it a reconditioning treatment each week. You can buy reconditioning cream in 2/6 tubes at most of the bigger chemists and hairdressers. Shampoo your hair before using the cream. This should make your hair healthy and shining again.' An advertisement in **Vogue**, July 1955, tackled the problem: 'Straggliness between perms? The Tao clinic specialises in hair conditioning through high-frequency violet ray – 8/6 for a fifteen minute treatment.'

Once the perm was done, there was little you could do to change the results except wait for it to grow out, so it was vital to consider the style carefully beforehand. Another sad reader of **Woman's Weekly** wrote: 'I had a new permanent wave three weeks ago and think I should have had my parting altered to the other side, as the hair has been getting rather thin here for some time. If I had it done now would it mean having some of the permanent wave cut away?' The response: 'Probably, if you altered your parting to the other side of your head. But if you merely had your hair parted a fraction of an inch higher or lower than the present one, only very slight trimming would be necessary. It is a very good plan to change one's parting every now and then.'

In between your four-monthly perms it was necessary to set your hair. Many women went to bed every night with a head full of pins, surrounded

**In the first style,** it was about two inches long; he set it loosely with the ends flicked away from her head to make her hair appear fuller and longer

by a headscarf. **Woman's Companion**, November 1958, recommended that while your bath fills: 'fasten your curls with pins and then tie up out of the way with a scarf. If you wish to give extra fullness to your style, set it over large rollers with a little cologne or quick setting lanolised lotion.' However, a Snowfire advertisement in August 1954 claimed: 'Twice a week is enough to pin your curls and put new life in your old perm, no need to bristle with pins every night, even though your perm's getting old or your short crop is growing out. Simply set with Snowfire – once after shampooing then before a midweek occasion. And of course if your hair is right on form, a single set with Snowfire will keep it obediently lovely throughout the week. Just run your comb quickly through your hair after setting with Snowfire and see how curls spin into place!'

On the other hand, the **Academy of Charm and Beauty** commented that: 'Rolling your hair up in curls is a nightly beauty routine in homes all over the country, for most women realise they look much better with a well-placed curl.' The advice continued with detailed instructions for putting in the curl: 'There are two general methods of placing that curl – the roll-it-up-in-a-curler method and the pin curl. Each gives good results if you know which to use for which hair-style. Generally, curlers give a tighter curl, pin curls a more natural wave. There are certain "do's" and "don'ts" to using curlers properly. For instance, don't roll up your hair when it is dripping wet. The curls will be too tight.

**The second style** was done six weeks later when Jane's hair had grown about an inch and a half. This time he set it all on rollers to raise it away from her head and give it plenty of body. And the lifted top hair gives her face the extra height it needs

▲ Advert, 1958. Cutting children's hair at home had moved on from the pudding basin.
◀ Very windswept styles, especially the one on the left.

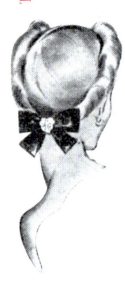

▼ Long and short styles, but in both, the emphasis is on youth.
▶▲ Hair bands from 1959 – you begin to see the 1960s coming.
▶▶ In 1959, hair bands became the height of fashion.

'Part your hair off in sections and make sure you place the curler at the tip of the strand of hair. To do this, start with the curler mid-way on the strand of hair and push it down to the tip. The reason you roll from the very tip is to avoid "fishhooks".

'Using a "rat-tailed" comb, tuck in all stray ends around the curler as you wind up the hair. Wisps of hair sticking out here and there do not make for a neat coiffure. Roll loosely to avoid any frizzing.

'Now, if you wish to make pin curls the hair may be somewhat damper than for curlers. In making pin curls it is important to divide the hair into smaller sections than you do when using curlers. The strands of hair to be used for the curls must be uniform in size, and each strand must be cleanly separated from the rest of the hair.

'You can make natural looking waves with pin curls if you start each curl near the scalp and wind in ribbon-like fashion. By that I mean wind the hair around the finger without twisting or turning the strand. Roll each curl with the hair ends in the centre. Don't let stray ends stick out.

'Pin each curl close to the head, not on top of the next strand you must pick up to form another curl. Pin each curl carefully so as not to spoil its roundness.

'And for best results all the curls in one row should face the same way – in the direction you want the hair to go when you comb it out. Curls can be held in place with one bobby pin or two hairpins.

'Naturally, if you take thick strands of hair you may need more pins to hold the curls. If you plan to sleep on the pin curls, bobby pins probably will hold more securely.'

There was a plethora of hairstyles to choose from, ranging from the short gamine or urchin cut, as worn by Audrey Hepburn, through the perennial mid-length cut sported by Marilyn Monroe to the long, shoulder-length hair of Diana Dors, and variations of each, such as the French pleat or the puffed-up style known as the 'chrysanthemum cut'. **Woman's Weekly**, January 1952, had some creative suggestions: *'Something new in the way of hairdos for those whose hair is short or in the growing stage. Brush the sides loosely back in a roll to a point in the nape of the neck. Put in a few pins to hold the shape at the base of the roll and slide in a comb to which a black velvet bow has been sewn. For evening – clip your rhinestone brooch into the centre of the bow.'*

**Everywoman**, June 1955, advised: *'If you're going to wear an ornament in your hair, take it to your hairdresser so that he can create your style around it. If you have your hair done and stick a rose on it afterwards, it will look wrong because you will have spoilt the balance.'*

From **Woman's Weekly**, September 1954: *'This style will suit any girl who likes her hair short but not looking severe. The simple effect is obtained by clever cutting so that the softly sculptured curls fall easily into place after setting.*

*'The crown and top of the head are combed smooth. Both sides are pinned in matching directions and the front piece of hair is turned forward to form a high curl on the forehead.'*

1) The side view of the "pli" showing the pinning of the curls above the forehead and the alternate directions in which the side curls are placed.

2) The back of the "pli". from the centre back the curls are turned in opposite directions, each row of curls being different from the one above.

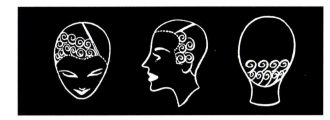

Hairstyles directed at the teenage market, such as the pony-tail, began to appear from the middle of the 1950s: *'A delightfully casual style for the young girl with a round face. The hair is parted at the side slanting towards the crown. To comb it out: brush the front wave into shape, and let the short ends on the sides fluff softly. The back is worn in loose, casual curls. Brush the sides into a deep forward wave ending in a hook curl'*, **Woman's Weekly,** March 1958.

The 'plis' for the style pictured above, show how to set the pin curls on the front, side and back of your head. The French twist and the bob appeared, to be followed in 1958 by wildly coloured, bouffant hair, false eyelashes and pale tones of foundation.

By the end of the 1950s fashionable women were wearing their hair fairly short, about chin level, with the whole effect being fairly natural, slightly windswept and with a soft wave. Often this style was worn with a hairband or a variation, the 'vamp band' after its inspiration from the 1920s.

**Woman's Weekly**, August 1958, told its readers that: *'A too curly or frizzy effect is now dated. A soft, casual-looking style is younger, more contemporary, and neat as you please for all its easy look.*

*'A narrow face needs widening. This can be achieved by a style which has side "wings" over the ears and a fringe brushed to one side. The eyebrows should be lengthened with pencil and plucked across the bridge of the nose.*

*'A round face needs height so the fringe is turned back in pompadour style with a few wispy ends curled down towards the forehead. Brows should be arched to break the round lines of the face.*

*'Both these styles feature medium-length hair, set in loose easy waves and curls. If you have no natural curl in your hair, a light permanent wave will ensure a tidy,*

▼ Hairstyle from 1959 – the style of the early 1960s has arrived.

well-groomed appearance at all times, and in any weather.

'Remember that your all-over size and proportions should be taken into consideration when choosing a style. A petite girl looks swamped in a bouffant bob and a tall, big-boned girl equally out of place with a dainty feather cut', **Woman's Weekly**, August 1958.

'If you're not satisfied with your hair as it is, add a hair-piece. A good hair-piece is made of real human hair, most of which comes from the Balkans.

'Be sure to have colour and texture matched exactly. A master blender can match it expertly, if he has a sample strand before him.

'Most switches have specially designed devices that pin them on to stay forever.

'Artificial braids are versatile. They adapt to your way of life, your hat, the time of day, the nature, length and thickness of your hair – possible combinations are numerous. Simple but effective, the chignon braid can lend distinction to very plain and otherwise unattractive hair, it makes an ideal career-girl special.

'Take good care of your braids. They need cleaning as often as your hair needs shampooing. And if hair is light, more often then when dark. At any rate, don't treat the braids like a hat which may not get cleaned for seasons on end.

'"Artificial" hair should be dry-cleaned with a reputable dry-cleaning fluid. The braid should be opened, combed and then dipped into the solution. Dry-cleaning revives lustre. Tints should not be used. Daily combing removes surface dust', The **Academy of Charm and Beauty**.

## Men's Hair

As they had done for many years, at the beginning of the decade both boys and men went to the barber once a month and had a 'short back and sides'.

With the growth of teenage fashions, this began to change. 'Spikey-tops', or crew cuts, became popular with younger men in the late 1940s as an accessible way to look American – you might not be able to get the clothes, but you could have the haircut.

An alternative was to grow the hair long on top, where it was held in check with copious amounts of cheap dressing. A correspondent to **Men Only**, April 1952, complained: 'I want expensive toilet soaps and shaving lotions and hair creams (not a fourpenny tin of petroleum jelly which makes my hair look like sucked treacle toffee).

From this the DA– 'Duck's Arse' – evolved, extravagantly quiffed. For many younger men the answer was some kind of compromise: a bit longer round the back and sides than had been the case, as long on top as your boss, or your mum, would let you get away with, and the same for the sideburns. Styles varied, according to your favourite film stars or music stars: Tony Curtis – a sharp, Italian look, Tommy Steele –

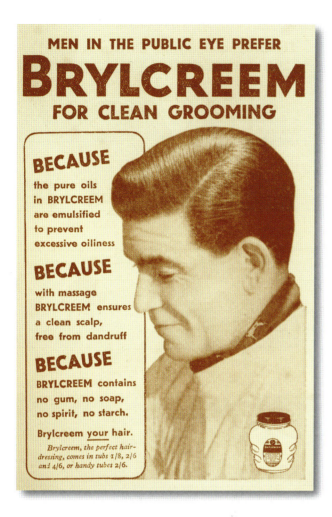

MEN IN THE PUBLIC EYE PREFER

# BRYLCREEM
## FOR CLEAN GROOMING

**BECAUSE**

the pure oils
in BRYLCREEM
are emulsified
to prevent
excessive oiliness

**BECAUSE**

with massage
BRYLCREEM ensures
a clean scalp,
free from dandruff

**BECAUSE**

BRYLCREEM contains
no gum, no soap,
no spirit, no starch.

Brylcreem your hair.

*Brylcreem, the perfect hair-
dressing, comes in tubs 1/8, 2/6
and 4/6, or handy tubes 2/6.*

In the early 1950s, men's hair was kept in place by copious amounts of dressing, such as Brylcreem.

Tommy Steele – music and film stars influenced teenagers' hairstyles.

Vaseline hair tonic advert – by the middle of the decade hairdressing was done with a gentler touch, 1955.

**Handsome hair** when you check Dry Scalp

Let's face it — healthy hair is handsome hair. Oil-starved roots and Dry Scalp just won't let your hair have that neat and natural, well-groomed look.
A few drops of 'Vaseline' Brand Hair Tonic, massaged gently into the scalp each morning, will check Dry Scalp, supplement the natural scalp oils and promote healthy, neat, and handsome hair. Why not let 'Vaseline' Hair Tonic help *your* hair to be its natural, good-looking self? Buy a bottle today.

Dry, scruffy hair? Hair that is hard to manage? Your trouble is probably Dry Scalp. Check Dry Scalp by massaging daily with 'Vaseline' Hair Tonic.

THE DRESSING THAT CHECKS DRY SCALP

Just twenty seconds every morning and see the difference! 'Vaseline' Hair Tonic supplements the natural scalp oils, keeps hair *naturally* handsome.

**Vaseline** HAIR TONIC

extravagantly long and bushy on top, Elvis, and his British counterparts, Cliff Richard or Marty Wilde – versions of the DA and sideburns.

As with clothing, the younger styles slowly worked their way upwards through the age brackets. Softened versions of younger styles appeared, especially the shorter-topped, slightly longer-sided Italian look of Tony Curtis.

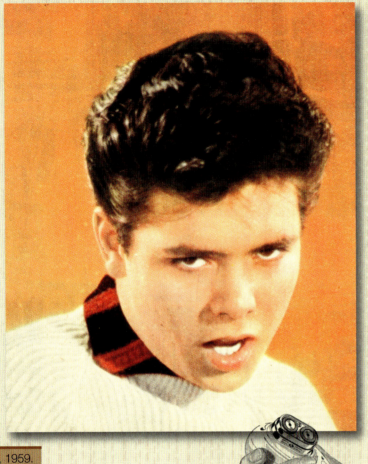

clipper head that would 'trim your moustache, "side-boards" and neck hair'; and all for £8 19s. The interesting thing about this shaver was that the shaving head was at one end of the razor and the clipper head at the other! Alternatively, **Men Only** that month recommended an electric dry-shaver powered by three 1½ volt batteries, which would give you six weeks shaving, or you could plug it into the dashboard of your car – cost £9 18s.

After-shave lotion was beginning to be more widely accepted, especially by the young, though many older men still viewed those who wore it with some suspicion!

This is the shaver with Rotary Action. Its blades rotate to shave bristles growing in all directions, to shave them without pulling or scraping, to shave them in complete comfort. And the raised rim gently smoothes out the skin so the blades can get right down to the job. This, in fact, is the world-famous **PHILISHAVE** —the scientific dry shaver that must give you a closer shave in comfort.

Dual-volt model AC/DC 110-130v 200-250v.
Stand-volt model AC/DC 200-250v.
Battery model (works off three 1½v. batteries)

£7·11·9 (tax paid)
£6·16·0 (tax paid)
£7·11·3 (tax paid)

OR ON EASY PAYMENT TERMS
A PRODUCT OF PHILIPS ELECTRICAL LIMITED

▲ Cliff Richard, 1959. By the end of the decade, men's hair-styles were following a softer, shorter, more Italian style.
▶▲ Philishave electric razor, 1958.
▶ Electric shavers were seen as acceptably modern, as this Remington from 1955.
▼ Toiletries for men were gradually, if somewhat grudgingly, being accepted through advertising like this, connecting them with manly pursuits such as rugby.

## Shaving

Beards remained the province of academics, bohemians and musicians. Jazz musicians and beatniks sported goatees, or a thin beard that ran round the line of the chin, with a clean-shaven face and neck, or which went into a version of the goatee.

Moustaches, usually trimmed to the line of the upper lip, were worn mainly by older men, although a very thin moustache might be seen, along with a cravat, a blazer and a cheese-cutter cap, on a more-than-slightly racy wolf-type.

The electric shaver, which had been around for some time, really came into its own during this time. In December 1955 the 'Richard Trim2Shave' was advertised as the world's only shaver that had, in addition to the normal shaver head, a

# The figure

*'The New Silhouette needs a New Figure. It demands above all, a figure to emphasise the smallest, neatest whisper of a waist that can be clasped between two hand spans', **Vogue**, 1949.*

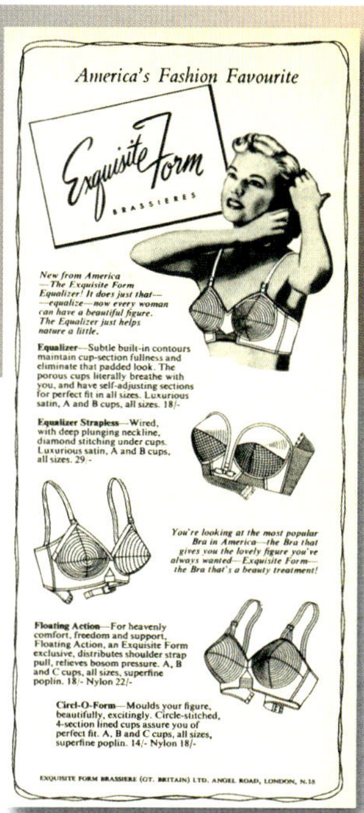


◂ The perfect 1950s figure – large breasts and hips and a small waist to create the 'hourglass' look.
▾ Weight and measurement chart for the perfect figure, from the **Academy of Charm and Beauty**, 1953.

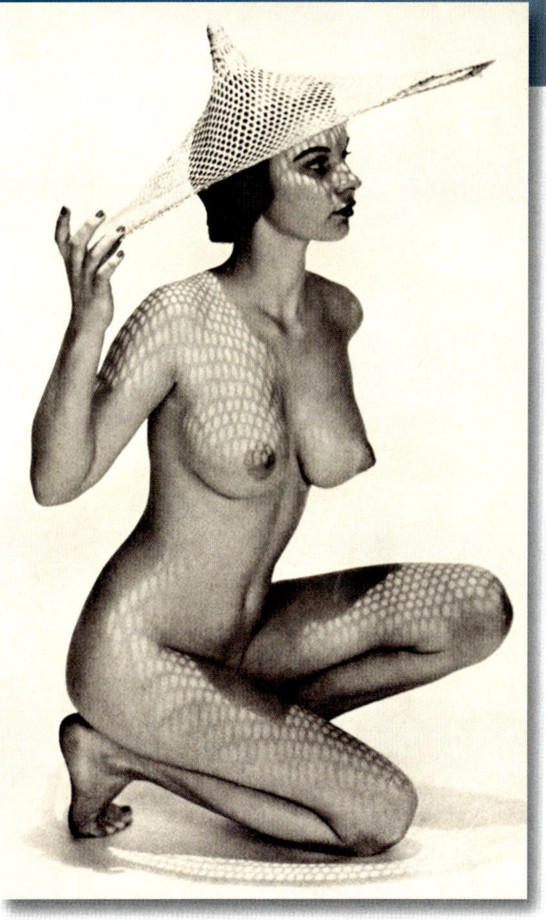

**During** the 1950s there evolved two very different fashionable shapes. On the one hand there was the gamine, a pretty urchin with a slight, half-starved figure epitomised by Audrey Hepburn. At the other extreme the new look transformed the female silhouette from the distinctly natural look of the war years into the hourglass shape, with its high rounded bust and tiny waist emphasised by hip padding and abundant skirts, as exemplified by Marilyn Monroe, with her ample figure and undulating walk.

A correspondent to **London Life**, May 1958, reported that: *'It seems to me that slim or tight skirts are being worn here and in America by girls who are slim enough to do them justice, but very few girls use the exaggerated wiggle of Marilyn Monroe, being quite content with the natural wiggle produced by a normal manner of walking.*

*'James Laver, the noted fashion historian, states that fashion goes in cycles from one point of interest to another and that after years of interest in the bosom, focus is now on the rear. This theory is well borne out by such stars as Marilyn Monroe and Diana Dors, noted equally as well for their ravishing derrieres as for their bosoms. Lately a Miss Vikki Dougan has ridden to success on the strength of a small part in "The Great Man", in which all she had to do was leave the room, the camera focusing on the swaying of her back view, which, needless to say, was clothed in the tightest of tight skirts. Later she appeared*

| Height | Age | Weight | Neck | Bust | Waist | Wrist | Abdomen | Hips | Thigh | Calf | Ankle | Arm |
|---|---|---|---|---|---|---|---|---|---|---|---|---|
| 5′ 0″ | 15–35 | 7 st. 2 lbs. | 11¾ | 31⅛ | 23⅝ | 5⅜ | 28 | 31½ | 18⅞ | 11⅝ | 7⅛ | 9⅜ |
| | 35–60 | 7 st. 6 lbs. | 11⅞ | 31¾ | 24 | 5½ | 28½ | 32¼ | 19⅛ | 11⅞ | 7⅜ | 9⅝ |
| 5′ 1″ | 15–35 | 7 st. 7 lbs. | 11⅞ | 32⅛ | 23¾ | 5½ | 28¼ | 32 | 19 | 12 | 7¼ | 9½ |
| | 35–60 | 7 st. 11 lbs. | 12 | 32⅝ | 24½ | 5⅝ | 28¾ | 32½ | 19¼ | 12⅛ | 7¾ | 9¾ |
| 5′ 2″ | 15–35 | 7 st. 12 lbs. | 12⅛ | 32¼ | 23⅞ | 5½ | 28½ | 32¼ | 19⅛ | 12⅛ | 7½ | 9⅝ |
| | 35–60 | 8 st. 2 lbs. | 12¼ | 32¾ | 24¾ | 5⅝ | 28⅞ | 32¾ | 19½ | 12⅜ | 7⅝ | 9⅞ |
| 5′ 3″ | 15–35 | 8 st. 3 lbs. | 12¼ | 32½ | 24 | 5⅝ | 29 | 33 | 19½ | 12¼ | 7⅝ | 9¾ |
| | 35–60 | 8 st. 7 lbs. | 12⅜ | 33 | 24⅞ | 5¾ | 29½ | 33¾ | 19¾ | 12½ | 7¾ | 10 |
| 5′ 4″ | 15–35 | 8 st. 8 lbs. | 12⅜ | 33¼ | 24⅛ | 5¾ | 29¼ | 33½ | 19⅞ | 12⅜ | 7¾ | 10 |
| | 35–60 | 8 st. 12 lbs. | 12½ | 33¾ | 25 | 5⅞ | 29¾ | 34½ | 20¼ | 12⅝ | 7⅞ | 10¼ |
| 5′ 5″ | 15–35 | 8 st. 13 lbs. | 12⅝ | 33¾ | 24¼ | 5⅞ | 29½ | 34¼ | 20⅛ | 12½ | 7⅞ | 10¼ |
| | 35–60 | 9 st. 3 lbs. | 12¾ | 34 | 25¼ | 6 | 30 | 35¼ | 20½ | 12⅞ | 8 | 10½ |
| 5′ 6″ | 15–35 | 9 st. 4 lbs. | 12¾ | 34½ | 25½ | 6 | 30 | 35½ | 20¼ | 12⅝ | 8 | 10½ |
| | 35–60 | 9 st. 8 lbs. | 12⅞ | 34¾ | 25⅞ | 6¼ | 30¾ | 35¾ | 20⅝ | 13 | 8⅛ | 10¾ |
| 5′ 7″ | 15–35 | 9 st. 9 lbs. | 12¾ | 35 | 26 | 6⅛ | 31 | 36 | 20¾ | 12¾ | 8⅛ | 10¾ |
| | 35–60 | 9 st. 13 lbs. | 13 | 35½ | 26½ | 6⅜ | 31¾ | 36½ | 21 | 13⅛ | 8¼ | 11 |
| 5′ 8″ | 15–35 | 10 st. 0 lbs. | 13⅛ | 36 | 27 | 6¼ | 32 | 37 | 21¼ | 13⅛ | 8½ | 10⅞ |
| | 35–60 | 10 st. 4 lbs. | 13¼ | 36½ | 27½ | 6½ | 32¾ | 37¼ | 21⅝ | 13½ | 8⅝ | 11¼ |
| 5′ 9″ | 15–35 | 10 st. 5 lbs. | 13½ | 36⅛ | 27¼ | 6⅜ | 33 | 37¼ | 21¾ | 13½ | 8⅝ | 11⅛ |
| | 35–60 | 10 st. 9 lbs. | 13¾ | 37 | 27¾ | 6⅝ | 33¾ | 37¾ | 22¼ | 13¾ | 8⅞ | 11½ |
| 5′ 10″ | 15–35 | 10 st. 10 lbs. | 13⅞ | 37½ | 27¾ | 6½ | 33½ | 37½ | 22⅛ | 13⅞ | 8¾ | 11⅜ |
| | 35–60 | 11 st. 0 lbs. | 14¼ | 38 | 29 | 6¾ | 34¼ | 38½ | 22¾ | 14¼ | 9 | 11¾ |

These measurements and weights are for the modern " streamlined " actress or model figure. For heavier-than-rage bone structure allow about seven pounds more and an inch for torso measurements. For very small bone icture, deduct five to ten pounds. For a well-proportioned figure, the bust and hip measurements should be about same and the waist-line about ten inches less. Within an inch or two—either way—is good.

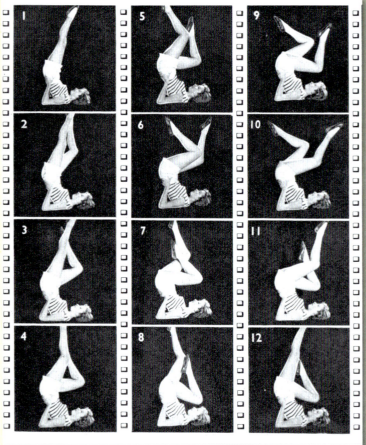

at a concert wearing a gown cut so low in the back that one critic referred to her as showing "her derrière decolletage".

'The Male has been divided by some authorities into three groups – leg men, bosom men, and admirers of the female derrière. The first two have had their innings and now it is the turn of the latter group. It is the tight skirt which gives connoisseurs of feminine beauty a visual feast. This neglected feature of the female anatomy is, to many, the epitome of beauty, the pinnacle of womanhood. Not only in motion but also standing still the slim skirt also does wonders for the perfectly shaped derrière. Whilst I am an admirer of the girl who wears the really clinging gown on the stage or screen, I do not advocate them for the average girl, as they are out of place. However, I do feel that the slim skirts these days are certainly most attractive and are a relief from the tight sweater days – the days of falsies and other pieces of sly engineering calculated merely to deceive the male. The only girls here who are wearing slim or tight skirts are those able to show to advantage those places which tight skirts show off so well.'

He was right in one sense; women's magazines advertised false busts made of sponge rubber at 10s 6d each – another correspondent to **London Life**, May 1954, wrote sadly that: 'On my honeymoon I was appalled to find that my wife wore one of those brassières that are blown up with a little tube, and that the figure I had so much admired owed more to artifice than to nature.'

But the idea that the new fashions made such engineering a thing of the past is highly dubious. **Glorify Yourself**, in 1953, stated: 'Fashions today

▲▲ The ultimate male – his legs are far more worked on than his 1940s predecessors.

▲ Ryvita advert, 1955. Exercises would help you achieve the perfect shape.

▶ Adverts offered ways to change your shape, lose weight, gain weight etc.

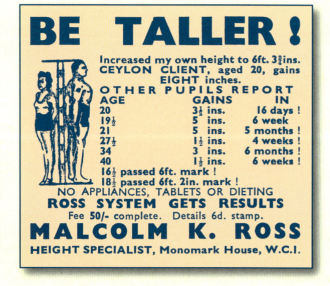

make women even more figure conscious than ever before. Some women take the attitude that nothing can be done about what may be wrong with their figures. But they are mistaken, for the expert dress designer has laws for every possible figure defect.

'Clothes can be made to give the appearance of a streamlined figure, they can trick the eyes into not seeing the faults. Long necks, short waists, wide hips – all can be skilfully concealed or camouflaged by the right kind of clothes.'

In all fairness, the fashions of the day did dictate a very rigid idea of the correct shape a woman should be. For the ideal shape: 'The largest part of the bust should equal the largest part of the hips and the waist should be ten inches smaller than either. That means that with a 36 inch bust, ideally the largest part of your buttocks should measure 36 inches, and your waist should be 26 inches', while 'You're considered short if you're under five feet two. Your height is considered normal if you're between five feet two and five feet six. And you're considered tall if you're over five feet six', the **Academy of Charm and Beauty**, 1953.

By the end of the decade, the fashionable female figure had considerably softened; the bust was smaller and rounder, the waist, while still accentuated, was less severe and the shoulders more curved.

To achieve the right shape there was slimming, with the help of products such as Ryvita crispbread and PLJ (pure lemon juice), but the fashion for a tiny waist created other problems for most women. One reader's letter to **Woman's Companion**, December 1958, asked: 'How can I reduce my waistline without making the rest of me thinner?' Exercise was the answer, and the magazine recommended the following: 'Lie flat on your back on the floor, arms stretched out flat on the floor, too, and then raise your legs so that they are at right-angles to your body. Put something such as a ball between your feet, and holding on to this, swing your legs first over to the right side, up again and then over to the left. Repeat ten times, two or three times a day if you can manage it. It is a tip-top exercise for waist-whittling.'

More advice for a trim waist included this aimed specifically at the many female clerical

workers whose day was largely spent sitting down: 'When you walk do you try to touch the ceiling with your head? Get all the walking exercise you can, but try these sitting down exercises too. Sit straight and pull those tummy muscles in as far back as they will go. Do this often. A second exercise to do at home is to clasp your hands on your lap and bend your body forward while throwing back your head.

'If you are faithful to these exercises you should soon notice a marked improvement. Once you have neatened your figure you will know how to keep it that way.'

◄◄ An exercise belt for the perfect figure in just 5 minutes a day!

◄ Adverts offered ways to change your shape.

▼ An end to having sand kicked in your face – Charles Atlas!

**Woman's Weekly**, May 1954, gave other advice for sedentary clerical workers: *'Take up dancing. There is nothing like it for neatening the hip line. It is so good for one's posture, too, and brings a new grace of movement with it. Take dancing lessons if you need them and practise your steps at home for fifteen to twenty minutes daily with the radio as your accompanist.'* **Woman's Companion**, November 1958, announced: *'the latest craze – the Hula Hoop game. Youngsters do it for fun, while grown ups do it to slim. It's a wonderful way to shed unwanted inches on the waist and hips.'*

**Ryvita** adverts regularly included exercises, such as this one from August 1954, for reducing the hips: *'Arms up and over your head (keep them in line with your ears, please). Now forwards and down as far as you can go, knees tensed and weight on your toes. Contract your buttocks and up you come. Repeat this 16 times.'*

Here's an exercise from **Woman's Companion**, October 1958, for the chest and back: *'Stand erect and raise arms to shoulder level, bending elbows so that your hands are in front of your shoulders. Using only the muscles in your shoulder blades, pull your shoulders back as far as you can. Relax and repeat rhythmically.*

*'Take a stick some three or four feet long, grasping it at each end and holding it above your head. Then lower it so that it rests across your shoulders. By degrees place your hands nearer together so that more and more muscular effort is used in doing this exercise.'*

Other exercises were more general, such as these from **Woman's Own**, February 1954: *'Winter's the time we put on weight – not enough exercise and starchy foods are often the cause. A few minutes a day spent doing simple exercises, though, will keep your figure trim and tone up your muscles. For the good of your whole silhouette – hips, stomach, thighs and upper arms – try this one. Lie flat on the floor, body stiff and arms folded over your chest. Roll slowly over on your left side and then right over until you are lying on your stomach. Return to starting position. Repeat to right side.*

*'Continue this rolling, first to the left and then to the right, for five minutes by the clock. Air-cycling is another excellent way of keeping the body shapely and firm.'*

However, there were downsides to exercising, as **Everywoman**, March 1951, reported: *'Over-exercise can give you ugly, knotty muscles that cramp easily. Ballet-dancers who have over-trained bear witness to this.'*

The face and neck also needed work. The **Academy of Charm and Beauty** recommended: *'Patting under the chin with the backs of the hands can break down the weight in the face, dispersing the fatty tissue.'* **Woman's Companion**, November 1958, gave advice for avoiding a double chin: *'I expect you know that too high a pillow and bad posture can have their effect on the chinline – so be sure to sleep as low as you can and when reading, hold your book or paper up rather than let your chin droop. Cream your chin at bedtime to keep the skin supple and once daily, if possible, soak a pad of cottonwool in skin tonic, place under the chin and bind in place with a bandage taken over the top of your head. Leave for half an hour, then remove and give a little brisk tapping with the backs of your fingers.'*

**Tatler**, February 1956, suggested: *'Place the fingers of each hand just underneath the cheekbones close in to the*

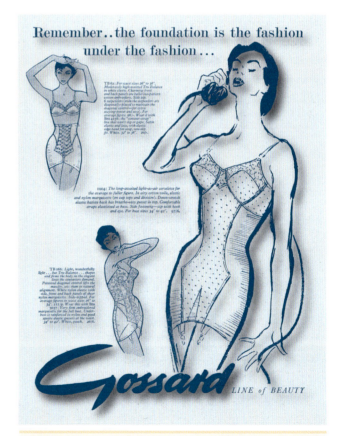

◄ An electric massager to help you smooth away the unwanted flesh.

▲ Heavy corsets could squeeze you into something like the perfect shape. Just about all women, from early teenage, wore a foundation garment.

CORSETIERE

"FRIGHTENING WHEN YOU THINK OF WHAT LIES AHEAD"

*'Next you must deal with the contours and for this put a little cleansing cream on your fingers so that they slip easily for the particular form of massage which is to follow. Grip the chin on either side, with the thumbs on top and fingers underneath. Now rub briskly along the jawbone up to the ears, pressing the jawbone firmly with the first fingers of each hand, which are pressing up from beneath. The best way to do this is to rub*

*nose – and do a brisk rotary movement, pressing well in so that you feel the muscles moving under your fingertips. Move a little further out and do the same thing again. Continue until you get right to the ears. Do not forget the forehead. Deep massage here relieves tension and stimulates circulation round the eyes. Place the fingers of both hands firmly on the bridge of the nose, and do a rotary movement all along the arch of the brows working out towards the temples.*

**STYLE 3**
★ *Wraparound Girdle. Full length hookside fastening*
**50/-**

**STYLE 2**
★ *Step-in Girdle with ¾ length zipper* **42/-**

**STYLE 1**
★ *Light weight Roll-on for the young figure* **30/-**

*first along one side and then the other, turning your head to the left and the right as you do so. The actual turning of the head is in itself a help, since the quick movement braces the muscles and stimulates the circulation. It is excellent, too, for the neck, and helps to keep the column round and firm.'*

However, in spite of all her best efforts, the 1950s woman still needed foundation garments. The **Academy of Charm and Beauty** was very firm about this: *'Every woman or girl, no matter how thin, should wear a girdle. Our finest designers insist that their slimmest models must wear girdles.*

*A man in your position*

Hungry . . . but no bread, no potatoes, no sugar, no wine. Very soon it may be just no . . . no . . . no . . . Do you struggle with yourself and then relapse? All this vain effort makes you irritable and tired but does *not* make you slimmer. Try an easier way, guaranteed for good results. The free Linia Booklet will tell you how.

# LINIA BELTS

Free Booklet on the Linia Method from Department B.18 at the address below:
Sold only by
**J. ROUSSEL LTD.** 177 Regent St. London W.1 Tel: Regent 7570
and at Aberdeen, Birmingham, Bristol, Leeds, Liverpool, Manchester, Glasgow, Nottingham

◀▲ To create the perfect figure corsets were real feats of engineering, verging on instruments of torture, as is reflected in this cartoon from **Everywoman**, March 1951.
▲ Corsets, 1954.
◀ For those who failed to look like Adonis, there were always aids.

'Wear a pantie girdle if you are slender; a pantie girdle with an open crotch if you are heavier; or a girdle with boning if you are definitely overweight.

'On the whole, your figure will look more youthful and you will protect your breasts from sagging by wearing a brassière and girdle and not a one-piece foundation garment.' **Everywoman**, February 1958, advised mothers on buying a foundation garment for their teenage daughter: 'Buy a cleverly cut roll-on that gives support without constricting your daughter and remember that when she leaves school and no longer has daily exercise, her muscles can become flabby, so support is essential.' She should also ensure that her daughter changed her roll-on once a week!

**Woman's Weekly**, July 1954, made the following recommendations: 'Figure is the first thing (apart from face and hair), so let's begin with a really good elastic belt and brassière. The belt must be the best you can afford, and then it will last. (You must budget ultimately for three, so that one is on, one for the wash, and one resting.) Be properly fitted in a good store, and be quite sure to get a belt with a high waist. This will do magical things for your figure and keep you permanently trim.

'Once you are right with belt and brassière (which must also be fitted), anything you put on will look well, even your old clothes while you are saving (two bras will be enough).'

**Everywoman**, March 1951, agreed that: 'You will get the soundest advice from a professional fitter in any large store which has a good corset department. You will probably find that a one-piece corselet will give you the best line, and this will be very comfortable to wear providing you get it the right length from bust to waist and have it in a flexible material which will stretch with every movement.

'If your figure is really heavy, your fitter may suggest a strong supporting belt with a deep bra which fastens over the top of it.'

The fashion for soft, curving lines, which accentuated the bust and hips, and a tiny waistline ensured an enormous boom in foundation

**It's simply wicked what it does for you**

Care to be daring, darling? To look outright naughty, yet feel downright nice? You'll get all the best lines . . . all the admiring looks—in your most demanding clothes. Your entrances? Positively breathtaking. Once you taste the spotlights and applause, you'll never go anywhere *important* without your Merry Widow.

STYLE 1311 6 gns and 1316 6½ gns both in black or white embroidered nylon marquisette. *Write today for illustrated brochure to : Warner Bros. (Corsets) Ltd., Dept. No. H4, 40/41, Conduit Street, London, W.1.*

**WARNER'S**
LE GANT
*Merry Widow*
*American designed Bras, Girdles, Corselettes*

*At all good stores including : LONDON Dickens & Jones Ltd., Marshall & Snelgrove Ltd., BIRMINGHAM Doris Floyd Ltd., BOURNEMOUTH Bobby & Co., Ltd., BRIGHTON Hanningtons Ltd. BRISTOL J. F. Taylor & Co. Ltd., CARDIFF James Howell & Co., Ltd., NEWCASTLE-UPON-TYNE John Moses & Co., Ltd., NOTTINGHAM Griffin & Spalding Ltd., SOUTHSEA Handleys Ltd.*

▲◄ Corsets for men, although the word isn't used.

◄ The sweater-girl bra, designed to give you the perfect pointed breasts.

▲ The 'Merry Widow' corset, 1956.

▶ For a brief period bras gave a more natural line, but they soon became part of a highly engineered foundation.

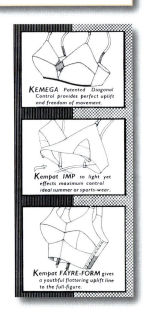

KEMEGA Patented Diagonal Control provides perfect uplift and freedom of movement.

Kempat IMP so light yet effects maximum control ideal summer or sports-wear.

Kempat FAYRE-FORM gives a youthful flattering uplift line to the full-figure.

garments. In 1950 the elasticated cotton roll-on was introduced. This was a girdle with suspenders attached; it superseded the boned and padded corsets previously worn.

However, later silhouettes – the sheath dress, the gamine look or the pneumatic Marilyn Monroe curves – placed impossible demands on the average female figure. Foundation garments, loose and practical in the 1940s, became feats of light engineering, to help the wearer to achieve a slim waist and hips or the large pointed bosom of Monroe or Jane Russell. Soft lines were achieved by corsets and bras, and adverts for underwear were everywhere.

A bra was also necessary, even for the youngest of teenagers. **Everywoman**, February 1958, gave advice to mothers: *'A teenager's bra must not be constricting. Look for a design that incorporates elastic insets at the front and sides and make certain the bra fits well. Freshness is all-important to her. See that she changes her bra daily (better buy three in nylon or cotton). And do be tactful, because secretly your daughter may be very self-conscious about her new appearance.'*

In France the fashion was for soft, rounded breasts, while in Britain the preference was more for the large Marilyn Monroe bust; bras were generally pointed, the effect achieved by the use of a mixture of cotton and nylon. The 'sweater girl bra' of the early 1950s had rows of concentric circular stitching on the cups to give them shaping. Also popular were decorative deep-waisted brassieres embracing both ribs and hip bones, called bustiers in France and rechristened 'Merry Widows' in Britain.

Foreign travel was a luxury at the start of the decade, so a good tan was almost a status symbol. The **Academy of Charm and Beauty** recommended that you should: *'Be sure you oil your body before exposing it to the sun. But any woman over twenty-five should not expose her face or neck to the sun for more than three minutes at a time. She can get all the healthful benefits she needs from the sun by lying with her face and neck under an umbrella or in the shade but with the*

◀ Another advert offering to give you the perfect shape.
▼ A sun-ray lamp was a cheap alternative to a foreign holiday for a tan.

▲ An interesting idea that resurfaces every so often.

▼ Plastic surgery advert, from 1950.

rest of her body exposed. If there isn't any protection for the face and neck around, spread a bandana, handkerchief, scarf, or anything you can find, over your face and neck. The sun's reflection is strong enough to give you an even tan.' And you could always cheat, as this advert from November 1955 recommended: *'Keep your "autumn gold" all through the winter with the Penetan ultra-violet sun lamp.'*

In an age where the rich had servants, the middle class, labour-saving devices, and the poor still did the weekly wash by hand, having good-looking hands was also a status symbol; *'I do a lot of cooking and preparing vegeta-*

bles and fruit often stains my fingernails a horrid grey; can you suggest treatment? – The best antidote is lemon juice; even the used skins will help.' **Everywoman**, February 1958, made suggestions for strengthening nails that had a tendency to split: *'Take a teaspoonful of powdered gelatine dissolved in a small glass of fruit juice once a day, preferably before a meal.'* **Woman's Companion**, December 1958, advised: *'Prepare your fingertips before using cuticle remover – this makes all the difference; just soak them in a bowl of hot, soapy water for about five or six minutes. Then quickly dab your fingers dry and swiftly run some cuticle remover round each nail base, using an orange stick wrapped with cottonwool. Leave this for two or three minutes, then using the blunt end of your orange stick, gently work back each cuticle in turn. Give a final rinse before drying your hands.'*

As with the perm, it was thought necessary for nails to be done professionally from time to time: **Everywoman**, March 1951, suggested: *'Have your nails professionally done once a month, after which, file them a fraction each night. In this way you keep the shape the manicurist has given you and also get rid of the start of splits and hang-nails before they have time to get serious. If, however, your nails are split from ill-health you should see your doctor, and also take a course of calcium.'* However: *'You'll have corrugated nails for ever more if you dig your cuticles too vigorously with a metal file or sharp orange stick; the nail below the cuticle is very much alive.'*

Further, **Woman's Companion**, December 1958, suggested that while you gave yourself a manicure: *'rest each elbow on half a lemon. This, I find, whitens and softens the elbows. Also, when making up, I always take time to smooth a little cake make-up over my hands and arms. Hands made red from housework can look smooth and perfect this way.*

*'For whitening the nails, put a little soapy water in a small dish and add the same amount of 10 volume peroxide. Dip an orange stick tipped with cottonwool into the mixture and run this under the finger nails; then rinse in warm water.'*

# Make-up

*'It is a healthy sign for a woman to be a little vain about her looks. In fact it is a duty she owes herself and those round her to look as attractive as her time and money will allow,'* **Woman's Weekly**, *July 1952.*

**Woman's Companion** magazine, December 1958, suggested that women carry out a job a day: one day a face pack, another a complete manicure, another a shampoo and set and another such jobs as tidying up eyebrows and removing underarm hair: *'By the end of the week you'll find yourself looking and feeling a different person.'*

And what were the tools required for all this? **Woman's Weekly** suggested that the bare minimum in beauty aids was: powder base, powder, rouge, lipstick, skin food, hand cream or lotion, talcum powder, brilliantine and a good hair tonic, as well as a full-sized mirror: *'which can easily be fixed to the back of the bedroom door, if space is limited'* and an enlarging mirror on the dressing table for making-up.

The start of a good beauty regime was a bath. In 1953, the **Academy of Charm and Beauty** stated that: *'For a long time it was felt that a shower was as good for the skin as a bath. Today most authorities feel that a bath is more beneficial . . . you should bathe five minutes once in every twenty-four hours when you are almost completely submerged in lukewarm water. Work up a good, soapy lather and cover every part of your body. Rinse off, and use a body brush with the second lathering. Let the warm water out and add cooler water for the last half minute or so or duck in and out of a shower. This is allowing minimum time. It's better if you can plan from fifteen minutes to a half-hour.'* **Woman's Weekly**, August 1954, recommended the addition of bath oil: *'it gives the bath water a lovely fragrance and, at the same time, leaves a dry skin softer and smoother'.*

A nightly cleansing with cold cream was the next part of the regime. It was massaged all over the face, working it thoroughly over every part, then wiped off

gently with a new piece of equipment, the face tissue. Then a little more of the same cream was smoothed on and you were ready for sleep. If your skin was extra dry, then after cleansing a rich skin food was recommended. *'Remember when applying this cream to tap a little extra into the skin round your eyes and over your forehead, two places where it can so quickly crease into fine lines. As well as the cold-cream treatment at night.'*

**Woman's Own**, February 1954, advised that: *'In the morning rinse your face with warm, then splash lavishly with icy cold, water. Wonderfully invigorating – you'll sparkle the day through.'*

**Woman's Weekly**, August 1954, recommended pore grains: *'They are just the thing for dealing with those open pores over nose or chin which give the skin such a dull, grey appearance. You can give the treatment every night – pour a tiny heap of the grains into the palm of one hand and mix to a paste with water. Then rub the paste over the offending areas. Rinse carefully with cold water to remove it. – Price 4/6d.'*

Red-veined skin was to be handled as little as possible, being cleansed at night by wiping with a milky cleanser, followed by some camphor ice. During the day a protective

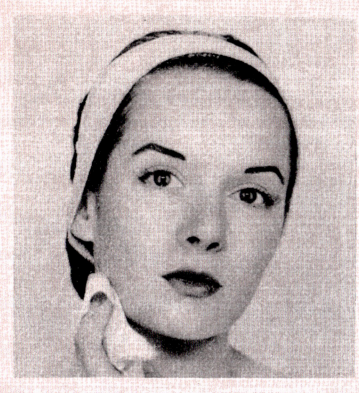

*Now pat dry with a face tissue.*

## Facial Mask

For a particularly flattering beginning to an evening out—especially if you've had a tiring day—cleanse your face thoroughly and then make yourself a cotton wool mask. Soak it in toning lotion, secure it round your face with crepe bandage or a long strip of linen, and leave it on for ten minutes while you relax with your eyes closed.

### How to make the mask

*Get a flat piece of cotton wool that's about 8 inches by 6 inches. Cut holes for eyes, mouth and nostrils, allowing quite large spaces for the eyes.*

make-up base and powder over it was recommended; if you had to be out of doors in hard or blustery weather, it was a good idea to use a little extra foundation and to finish with a powder-cream for added protection.

Now for the make-up. **Woman's Companion**, October 1958, suggested this be one of the first jobs of the day: *'Personally I think there's nothing like starting off the day nicely made-up. It takes only a few minutes – but these minutes become increasingly hard to find later in the morning and soon you find you've passed half your day without glamour!'*

First came the foundation, and this had to be chosen with care. There were three types of base: an untinted cream base, a tinted cream base, which gave a hint of colour to the skin, and a liquid-type base, which had previously been called 'liquid powder' and had been used only for the neck and arms, but by the early 1950s it had become suitable for use on the face, too. In July 1954, **Woman's Weekly** advised its readers on its use: *'Liquid foundations are best applied direct with the finger-tips . . . unscrew the cap and place your middle finger over the top of the bottle. Shake*

◀◀ Advice stressed that a clear complexion was the real foundation of good make-up, as with this advert for Pears soap, 1956.
▲ Making your own beauty facial mask.

*vigorously – to blend the liquid thoroughly with the colouring matter – then dot the make-up which is left on your finger over your face and neck. Blend quickly with both hands . . . remove any surplus with cotton-wool before you apply powder.'* The colour of the base needed to be neither too light nor too dark but a near match for your own skin colour.

Foundation was to be applied very carefully, right out to the hair line and over your neck and shoulders, particularly if you were planning to wear a low-cut dress. **Woman's Realm** suggested that: *'To get foundation really smooth, apply it with a spatula, dabbing specks lightly all over your face; blend it with little feathering strokes of your fingers.'*

All this took a lot of time and effort, as **Woman's Own** pointed out, February 1954: *'We all long for a roses-and-cream complexion, but oh! the time it takes to put on foundation, plus powder, plus again rouge – especially when you're in a frantic hurry to catch that train or bus. So, instead, use one of the new all-in-one powder foundations that take next to no time to apply. They're tinted, too, so away with your problems of looking colourless. One small word of warning: when applying, dab it with little swirls, moving in an upward direction. This way you'll get an even colouring.'*

Next came the rouge. The cream type was recommended for most skins because it blended easily and gave a lasting effect for six or eight hours. A cream rouge that went on smoothly was the best sort. If it wouldn't rub or slide through your fingertips, it was too heavy to put on your face. Powder rouge was useful for touching up make-up if you had not applied enough cream rouge to begin with, and also to renew make-up during the day. Cream rouge was to be applied just after the base, powder rouge after the face powder. **Woman's Weekly**, August 1954, suggested that: *'you try a special kind of rouge. It comes in a tiny stick so that you can place the smallest dot on each cheek to start with and as it is a very pale pink, it will not be difficult to achieve a natural effect. Like all cream rouges, it should go on over a foundation cream which will help you to blend it in.'*

**Everywoman**, March 1951, recommended: *'If you want to achieve the new lightweight look with rouge, apply it by pressing it on, rather than smoothing it over the skin. Cream rouge is better for this, and if the day is chilly apply it with warmed fingers.'* The **Academy of Charm and Beauty** warned: *'Remember that where rouge is concerned, the least bit goes a long way. It's better to have on too little than too much! The best over-all principle to apply to your rouge is, that you look unrouged. Blend the outside borders of the rouged areas until you cannot tell where the rouge starts or ends. This isn't easy, but once your skin has been moistened with a foundation, you will find the procedure simplified.*

*'The lighter the colour of your skin, the lighter should be your rouge. Match your rouge to your skin, more than to your eyes or hair, and one shade range is sufficient for every costume. Very often, a dusky-skinned blonde will have to use almost a brunette rouge to get the best effect. If you have very fair skin but dark hair and eyes, your rouge will be almost as light as a fair-skinned blonde's. On the whole, keep your rouge a soft and natural pink or red. Be wary of the freakish off-colours.*

*'Several times during the day you may wish to give your face a lift. Use a dry or cake rouge in the same place you applied the cream variety. Never try to apply cream rouge after you are once powdered. Dry rouge requires even more expert handling than the other types. Apply just a little and blend it in well, with your powder puff. The trouble is, as you rub it over, you move the colour from the middle area where you intended it. It's much better not to use it at all than to try to do a good job hurriedly.'*

Now for the powder: *'With a swan's down puff or piece of cotton wool press powder liberally all over your face and neck. Being generous with powder here is an economy – this way, you'll find it lasts hours longer. Now, gently dust off surplus powder, taking care to brush away every trace from hairline and eyebrows – use a little make-up brush, or cotton wool.'*

The **Academy of Charm and Beauty** also gave detailed advice on the application of powder: *'I once watched the late Monte Westmore, famous Hollywood make-up artist, powder*

*Vivien Leigh for her exquisite Technicolor scenes in Gone with the Wind. He used a piece of fresh cotton about five inches in diameter and very thick. He recommended that powder be shaken on to the puff to prevent its "packing". (This often happens when a woman presses the puff down into the powder box day after day for months. Transfer your powder to a talcum powder box, to a talcum powder jar or an old fashioned salt shaker.) Miss Leigh's hair was concealed, and every nth degree of skin on her face, neck, and behind her ears was thoroughly patted with powder. As he patted; he lightly pressed the powder into the skin. He often spent eight to ten minutes on this phase of her make-up alone. He insisted that there be no rubbing or smearing. Then he brushed her face and neck lightly, but thoroughly, with a powder brush. This is a brush made especially for this purpose. You brush in the direction the hair grows on your face, and continue until no one can see that you have used a trace of powder. You will notice that the brush bristles have a way of getting into wrinkles where the ordinary puff cannot reach. Once you have tried this almost magical powder technique, you can never be persuaded to go back to the old hit-and-miss method, with its conspicuous and unattractive results. And you won't have to powder very frequently during the day, either.'*

In December 1958, **Woman's Companion** gave tips on make-up for a party: *'When powdering, be rather more generous than usual. Press on lots and lots, removing the surplus with cotton wool, and then see what a lovely smooth look you will have achieved.'* In September 1954, **Woman's Weekly** explained how to avoid achieving a floury look after powdering – the secret was not to use: *'too light a shade of powder and one that does not blend sufficiently well with your skin tone. Try changing to a tinted foundation to give your skin an even film of colour and then use the powder which has the same shade name. (By the way your foundation should be just a little darker than your skin.)'*

Getting the right colour make-up was vital and **Everywoman**, June 1955, advised its readers: *'If you are wearing pastel shades, keep your complexion pale pink and white, but emphasise your mouth and eyes. Use a vivid pastel lipstick with a darker shade for outline. Darken your eyebrows if they're too fair, and use a little eyeshadow.*

*'If you wear grey, get plenty of colour into your*

▼ How you applied rouge depended on the shape of your face, as these four diagrams show.

### Long Face

A good tip is to smile and apply rouge to the cushions of the cheeks, keeping it well away from the nose. A touch of rouge on the chin helps to shorten the face.

### Round Face

Rouge should be applied high on the cheeks and near the nose, keeping the outer edges of the cheeks clear. This will minimize the roundness of the face.

### Square Face

Shape the rouge in faint triangles on the outer part of the cheeks, with the upright side of the triangle in line with the nose and the points towards the ears. This softens a too-strong outline.

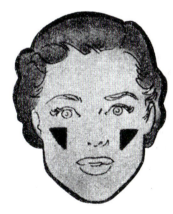

### Oval Face

Apply the rouge in a half circle near the eyes. This accentuates the classic shape of the face.

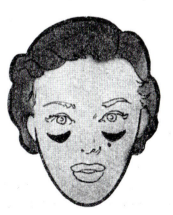

make-up – choose a slightly warmer foundation than usual, and a brilliant lipstick, and don't be afraid to use rouge if you need it. Only an exceptionally well-proportioned face can be successfully pale.

'Use a warmer foundation and powder for evening, and a darker red lipstick, because artificial lights drain away some colour. Match your foundation to the pigment of your skin – a pinkish one if you have a very fair skin, an apricot one if you have a creamy skin.

'Use dark powder to hide broken veins and high colouring, then powder over with your usual shade.

*Remove the surplus with a brush, or tissue. After about ten minutes powder again.'*

**Woman's Weekly**, July 1954, made the following recommendations: *'If you have sallow skin – do not use a yellowy powder. A pinky shade would be far more flattering. You could add a rosy glow by using a tinted foundation in the*

*same shade.'*

Next came the mouth. The lips were the absolute focus of attention in the early 1950s, and much advice was given on the subject. Whether you used a lipstick brush for applying lipstick or the stick itself, you were recommended to use small, feathery strokes to make sure that the lipstick clung well to the lips. Wholesale re-shaping of lips was to be avoided, but minor changes could be done. First, simply outline the shape of your lips. Then the first coat of lipstick should be reasonably light in colouring. If your hair was brown or black, a darker red than for blondes and redheads was suggested. If you were using a brush, it should be a genuine camelhair lipstick brush; a professional's brush with a long

▼ Make-up from 1955 – note how the lips have become fuller.

handle for home application, and in your bag a smaller one with a cover to protect the brush. Your lips should be perfectly dry. Then, to create an upward lift to the corners of your mouth, lips should be parted and colour applied at the inside of the upper corners with the brush saturated with the lipstick. Using small, curving strokes, gradually colour toward the centre of the upper lip. When you have completed one side of the cupid's bow, start at the other outside corner of the upper lip and work toward the centre. When the upper line is established fill it in, using plenty of lipstick, brushing it with up and down strokes to fill any crevices. Now begin on the lower line; start at the inside of the corner of the mouth, and continue along the natural line of the lower lip. Colour every bit of lip, and fill in as you did on the upper lip. Some make-up artists recommended that you show the bow on the lower lip. Let all the lipstick remain for a minute or so, then press a tissue between your lips and blot off as much colour as possible; repeat three or four times. This keeps some colouring on your lips all day or evening.

Confusingly, **Everywoman**, June 1955, advised: *'Fill out centre of mouth with lipstick, before using brush to outline – this gives you a guide to follow for the edge. If you cheat on the outline of your mouth, use a* *brush to do it.'* To avoid lipstick becoming caked as the day wore on, the advice was not to touch up existing lipstick, but to completely remove every trace and start again.

Once again, getting the right colour was most important and **Everywoman**, June 1955, suggested that: *'Very pale lips look all right with dark complexions, but they look strange with pale*

*English skins. And a pink lipstick easily becomes too diffuse. It needs a hard, clean outline, preferably drawn with a brush.'* The **Academy of Charm and Beauty** advised: *'if you are wearing a dress with orange colour in it, then select a*

▼ Bright-red lipstick is being joined by violets and purples, 1955.

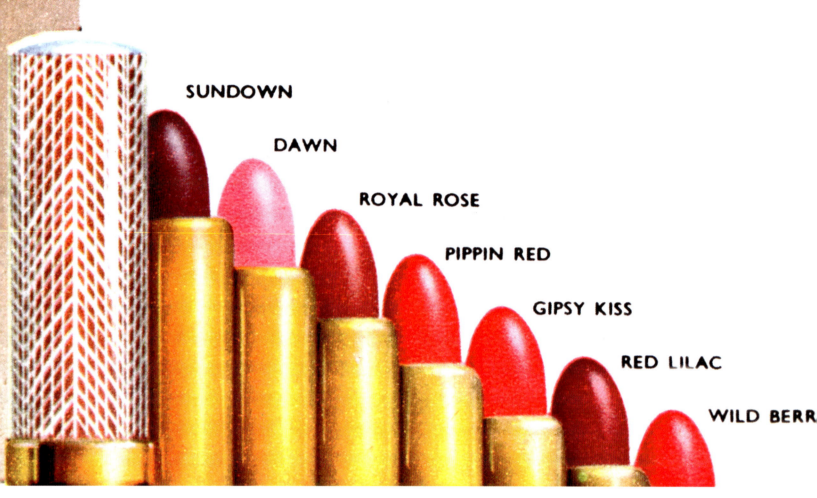

SUNDOWN

DAWN

ROYAL ROSE

PIPPIN RED

GIPSY KISS

RED LILAC

WILD BERR

*lipstick which has a definite yellow or orange tone. If your costume has a purple tone, select a lipstick with a cyclamen note like Atkinson's Tomboy. In other words, match your lipstick to your fashion shades with pastel colours. With clear reds, dark brown or greens a true red lip colour is essential. You must, therefore, keep several lipsticks of different shades, not just one colour to go with all your dresses. This whole technique takes a few extra minutes, but once you're finished you have a make-up which will stay fresh-looking for hours. It needs to be retouched only when you eat, or every four hours, so you needn't constantly be daubing at your lips.'*

**Everywoman**, March 1951, discussed some of the more popular lipsticks then newly on the market: Elizabeth Arden's 'Surprise' was *'more full-bodied than the pink-reds you've grown familiar with these last twelve months — it's a honey for brunettes, and beautiful with pale yellow and lime greens'*, and *'Coral Glow'* had *'a little more yellow in it and is fine for tweeds'*, while

*'Flamenco'* was *'a must for red-heads and would see a nicely-tanned blonde through the summer'*. Boots' *'Number 7 Tropic Tan'* was *'chic for a companion for navy-blue'* and *'Number 7 Fuchsia'* was *'good with blues of all tones, dark mauve and pink'*.

Lipstick could also be a problem as it would often get on the teeth. The **Academy of Charm and Beauty** gave clear instructions on how to avoid this: *'Owners of thin lips have the most trouble in this respect. An overdose of poorly applied lipstick may cause some of it, but on the whole it is formed by forming the consonants "f" and "v" incorrectly. Watch yourself as you say friend, fuss, vacant, vanity. Do your upper teeth close on the front part of your lower lip? Then it's easy to see why you get more than your fair share of lipstick on your teeth, isn't it. Instead place your upper teeth on the back part of your lower lip, where there is no lipstick. Your "f" and "v" are just as well enunciated — and you've cleared the lipstick area.'*

Another common problem was lipstick on clothes. **Woman's Companion** advised you to remove it by rubbing a little glycerine into the stain then leaving it for a little while before washing it out, having rubbed a little extra soap into the stain before washing.

In 1950 *'Gordon-Moore's Cosmetic toothpaste'* modestly described itself as the *'Most important beauty discovery since lipstick.'* It would *'rose-tint your gums to match your lipstick – as red nail varnish makes hands look whiter by contrast, so the rose-tint on your gums brings out the sparkling whiteness of your teeth'*! At 2s 6d it was quite expensive and very much aimed at women. However, Gordon-Moore's also catered for *'menfolk'* with *'Satin'* dental cream *'of the same high quality as the Cosmetic Toothpaste, but without the crimson colour'*.

Now for the eyes. **Woman's Weekly**, January 1952, asked: *'Are you careful to brush your eyebrows after powdering your face? Tiny particles of powder settle on your brows and, unless removed, give them a dusty appearance. The quickest and best way of removing powder is to smear the faintest trace of Vaseline over your eyebrow brush before you use it.'*

The shape of the brows was very important and this meant plucking. **Woman's Weekly**, August 1958, gave advice to those who found this painful: *'It sometimes helps to hold a flannel wrung out in hot water against the brows before plucking, then the hairs spring out more easily. Another trick to try is rubbing a menthol cone (buy this from your chemist) over the brows first. Pluck in the direction the hairs grow. This way they will come out more easily. Have a good pair of tweezers – the scissor type grips particularly well – grasp the hair as near the root as possible, then give one sharp tug. Remember you should remove hairs from beneath the brows always, leaving the natural line along the top untouched.*

*'The smartest women today have a natural brow line. The shape of your eyebrow should follow generally the upper curve of your eye. Avoid points on your brows. They are apt to give you a perpetually surprised look; they focus interest away from your eyes, and are unbecoming to most faces.*

*'Have an eyebrow brush almost the size of a toothbrush for your home brushing, and carry a smaller one in your bag. Brush your eyebrows up toward your forehead first and then brush them out toward your temples.'*

General advice was that if the eyebrows needed lengthening slightly or were not thick enough, the best thing was an eyebrow

◀◀ Make-up in 1958.
▼ Deep-red lipstick was the height of fashion in 1951.

# special make-up

**Eye-shadow** . . . blue or green frames need matching eye-shadow; with darker frames, use pale shadow. Carry make-up base right up to eyebrows, stipple shadow over lids, smooth out and up at sides. Powder to prevent crease marks, then add a second touch of shadow immediately above lashes

**Mascara** . . . apply quite heavily, then use lipbrush for fine eye-lining. Some lenses magnify eyes (and eye make-up), others diminish—with the latter, line bottom lashes as well as top, stopping two-thirds of the way in. Extend outwards with *downward* line—not parallel to upper extension line

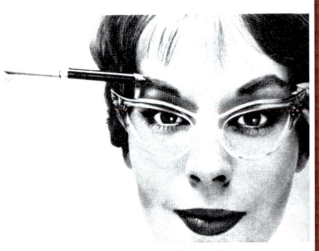

**Eyebrow pencil** . . . golden rule is to echo line of frame. Emphasize brows slightly along top, using light feathery strokes, and add a triangular point at top of arch. Extend brows slightly outward, with upward lift

pencil, sharply pointed for simulating the extra hairs. Or you might prefer to use a *'regular carbon drawing pencil'*. With either you should use small strokes about the length of a normal eyebrow to fill in or add to the desired line, *'never that single line from one end of the eyebrow to the other which is so hard-looking',* **Woman's Weekly.**

The **Academy of Charm and Beauty** recommended that: *'Most women must extend their brows about a quarter of an inch to the side, so that the brows give the appearance of framing the eyes. Be careful not to extend your brows down at the sides of your eyes, because any downward line is ageing. If your brows grow that way, naturally, you may find it wise to pluck a few of the lower ones and extend the pencil strokes out to the sides for correction.'* Alternatively, if the eyebrows were naturally well shaped and only needed darkening, this could be done very effectively with mascara.

As with everything else, colour was important. **Woman's Weekly** states: *'Use a black eyebrow pencil only if your brows are definitely black. Otherwise, a light brown for blondes or a dark brown for in-betweens and redheads is much more flattering. Smudge and soften eyebrow make-up by going over it with a brush or a tissue.'* **Vogue**, July 1955, advised its readers that: *'With holidays and swimming at hand, many women will like to try an eyelash and brow darkener that lasts for six weeks. Called Ciloreal, and made by L'Oreal, you simply apply one liquid, leave it on for two minutes, then apply a second liquid. Finally wash with soap and water. Made in dark brown only, the whole outfit costs 6/- from Boots.'*

The **Academy of Charm and Beauty** described another use for your eyebrow pencil: *'One of the most delicate bits of make-up to master is that of outlining the eyes with an eyebrow pencil. This is usually the same shade as you use on your eyebrows. Just as an etching often is improved by good matting and framing, so the eyes take on an interesting depth and apparently more size, when they are outlined. This will not show if it is done on that ledge of skin where the lashes grow. Do not put it above the lashes for then it will be too noticeable. Start your outlining at the middle of the upper and lower lids and extend out to the sides. By tracing a few dot lines in the form of a triangle from the corners of the eyes out towards the sides you can add still more size to the eyes. Don't underline small eyes – it makes them look smaller.'*

◄◄ Make-up for spectacle wearers, from **Woman** magazine, September 1958.
▼ Make-up in 1959.

The eyes became an increasingly important focus of make-up and mascara was widely used, but needed to be put on properly. The **Academy of Charm and Beauty**, 1953, advised: *'You will need to apply your mascara faithfully to both upper and lower lashes if they are very light, but otherwise concentrate on the upper lashes only.*

*'Two thin applications are much more efficient than one thick one. After two applications let the mascara "set" for a moment and then brush the lashes gently with a clean, dry brush to groom them thoroughly.*

*'The colour of mascara to use will depend upon your general colouring, and you should be careful not to use too dark a shade. Most blondes and redheads look best with dark-brown mascara. Preferably, only the darker brownheads and brunettes should use jet-black lash colouring. Some authorities say, "If the eyebrows are black, then and only then use black mascara."'*

**Woman's Weekly**, March 1959, suggested a simple trick for brushing on mascara: *'You tilt your head backwards for brushing the upper lashes, forwards when you do the lower ones. Try it next time you apply your mascara. It brings the lashes away from the surrounding skin and enables you to reach them more easily.'*

**Woman's Weekly** also suggested using two brushes: a damp one for applying the cosmetic and a dry one for separating the lashes. The first brush was to be dampened with hot water and used to brush the lashes up and back: *'This coaxes them to curl nicely'*. When the mascara had dried, a second, lighter coat was applied and allowed to dry. Finally, the lashes were separated with the dry brush, brushing up and back.

The **Academy of Charm and Beauty** declared that it was important to: *'Apply it to the lashes from the base to the tips. If your lashes are naturally dark, but perhaps sunburned or light at the tips, then apply the mascara to the end only.'* Then: *'When you remove the mascara make quite sure that the lashes are left scrupulously clean. A little Vaseline or cream on the lashes helps to keep the lashes soft and stimulates their growth.'*

**Everywoman**, June 1955, advised: *'Use black mascara to darken blonde eyelashes, then go over again with blue to soften the effect – surprisingly effective. Remove mascara splashes from your eyelids with a dampened wisp of cotton wool wound round an orange stick.'* While **Woman's Weekly**, March 1959, recommended that: *'Blondes look nicest in brown mascara for daytime, dark-blue for after-dark.'* **Woman's Companion**, December 1958, reported that: *'For special occasions, matching shades of mascara and eye shadow give a bewitching effect. Try mauve or green eye shadow and mascara for a change instead of the more usual brown or black.'*

Eye shadow had been regarded as definitely racy, but was gradually accepted, particularly for special occasions. Once again the **Academy of Charm and Beauty** had good advice for its application: *'With your finger-tip, apply the eye shadow to the outer half of the eyelid only, blending it upwards and outwards towards the temples until it fades completely. For evening, put a thin, emphatic line immediately above the eyelashes – it looks exceedingly pretty. If your eye sockets are shallow from brow to eyelid, lengthen the distance by keeping shadow well down the lid, away from brow.'*

**Woman's Weekly**, August 1958, advised its readers that: *'Used as delicately as the brush of a butterfly's wing, eye shadow gives depth and sparkle to your eyes as well as intensifying the colour.*

*'Eye make-up, like rouge, must be almost imperceptibly used to make you more attractive. If your eyes tend to bulge a little, cover your entire upper eyelid, up to the eye-brow line, with shadow. This will make your eyes look more deeply set. If, on the other hand, they look too deeply set, bring the foundation you use on the rest of your face right on over the lids. This will lighten the colour of your eye-lid and bring the eye forward. Shadow on the outer halves of the lids makes the eyes look farther apart. On the contrary, shadow on the inner half pulls them closer together, but this is very seldom necessary or attractive.'*

And the colour? **Everywoman**, June 1955, explained: *'Choose an eye shadow close to the colour of your eyes. But not brown, which is ageing and heavy, as the natural pigment of the eyelids is always darker than the rest of the face.*

*'Gold and silver eye shadows are exciting for evening – don't be afraid to use them sometimes. Greyish-green flatters nearly all blue-grey eyes.'* The **Academy of Charm and Beauty**, in 1953, expanded: *'For dark hazel, brown, or green eyes, use a blue-green eye shadow. For light hazel or grey eyes, use a blue-grey shadow; and for blue or grey eyes use either blue or blue-grey shadow depending upon the colour of your clothes.'*

Nails positively had to be varnished if you were to be fashionable, and there was a huge, ever-changing range of colours to choose from. In March 1951, one of the leading brands, **Cutex**, came in *'Ten gleaming colours – Confection Pink, Cotton Candy, Young Red, Prize Posy, Deep Rose, Star Bright, Pink Cameo, Colourless, Natural, Sheer Natural.'*

◄ Note the matching lipstick and nail varnish, 1953.

In March 1956, **Woman's Journal** advised that if your nails were short, you should paint them from base to tip, while if they were long, then the half moons should be left white. In December 1958, **Woman's Companion** advised: *'For party-wear, try one of the new delicate shades of nail varnish. There are some delightful colours in the palest green, mauve, blue and yellow. These colours should always be worn in tone with the shade of your dress.'* **Everywoman**, February 1958, suggested that for red hands, you should select a good bright red shade with no blue tones in it at all. A reader of **Woman's Own**, February 1954, shared a useful tip: *'Though I simply adore the pearl nail varnish, my wage does not allow me to buy a bottle in each shade. But I get a similar effect by using the clear pearl over most other pale shades.'*

Not only the finger nails were painted. Toe nails were also painted, previously a scandalous thing to do, but many women just did not have the feet for the fashion for open sandals in summer. As usual, the popular magazines gave instructions. *'You begin your pedicure either after your bath when the cuticles are softened or soak your toes in soapy water for ten minutes, then trim your toenails. Wrapping the pointed tip of an orange stick in cottonwool, dip it into cuticle remover and work this around the base and under the tip of each nail. After waiting for five minutes, work back the cuticle with the flat end of the stick, taking care not to force it back. If necessary repeat this treatment, until you get a perfect finish. A little cuticle oil applied regularly will keep the cuticles soft and pliable and you can work them back after bathing. Now they are ready for painting.'*

Post-war British women became more perfume conscious, and strangely this was probably because scent had been almost unobtainable during the war and was therefore highly prized. Whatever the reason, by the 1950s it

'Lanolite' Lipstick 7/9
('Non-Smear' and Regular)
'Wear-Longer' Nail Enamel 5/3

had never been so plentifully manufactured, and in so many forms.

First, and cheapest, were the toilet waters and perfumed colognes, lighter version of perfumes proper: *'use as lavishly and frequently as required, for they do not last as long as perfumes which they are not intended to replace'*.

Toilet water was meant to be sprayed on to the skin from an atomiser after bathing, when it would both *'refresh and scent the skin and also help it to cool and tauten, closing the pores and so contributing to health as well as glamour'*. **Woman's Companion**, December 1958, suggested that: *'A good plan is to keep this in the fridge if you have one, so that it is icy cold and therefore more invigorating. While you are at it, don't forget your feet, because, as you know, aroma always rises, and while you are dancing, you and everybody else will enjoy the fragrance as it wafts upwards.'*

Eau-de-Cologne has bergamot, an antiseptic, as one of its basic ingredients, so it not only has cooling and invigorating properties, but it can be used as a mouthwash, in the footbath and against infection. By the 1950s, many manufacturers were producing a cologne scented with popular perfumes.

Then there was perfume proper – how should it be applied? *'First, last and all the time, it must go on your handkerchief, the central point of diffusion. But except for that it should not be put on fabric, for it goes stale in time and gives clothes a musty smell, The only garments that will take it are furs. The hair, too, can be lightly sprayed.*

*'After this use it on the skin, All warm spots make good diffusers, which is why the ears are a favourite spot, but others are the crooks of elbows, backs of knees, fronts of wrists. But remembering what I said earlier, don't please put perfume on all available spots of your anatomy. For instance, neck and backs of knees would be good on the beach on your holiday; but arms and hair when you go dancing,'* The **Academy of Charm and Beauty.**

**Vogue**, in July 1955, announced that: *'Perfume in a new form has been introduced by Dana in the three famous fragrances of Tabu, Canoe, and Emir. The atomizer contains a combination of the perfume and a harmless gas. Pressure on a* button releases the finest possible spray of perfume which dries as it touches skin or hair. Because there is no alcohol (the gas takes its place), the perfume is potent and lasting. Price 35/-.'

◄◄ Revlon lipstick and matching nail varnish – pink was a particular favourite.
▼ Advert for Chanel, 1954. Some things don't change.
Over: Advert for Bond Street perfume by Yardley, 1953.

N°22
CHANEL
PARIS

THE MOST TREASURED NAME IN PERFUME...

CHANEL

# PRICE

## A short guide to typical prices from the period

## Clothes' Men

### General

Mentor sanforised shirts – from 17/6 (1953)
Old England shirts – £1.5.9 to £2.5.6 (1955)
Van Heusen Vantella shirt – £2.9.0 (1955)
Khaki drill trousers – 14/6 (1955)
Shetland socks 9½ to 12 inches – 11/- (1955)
Harris wool socks – 6/8 (1952) 7/- (1955)

### Coats

Gabardine raincoats, double-breasted – £5.17.6 (1953)
Plastic cycling cape – 14/11 (1953)
Men's Pakamac – from 17/6 (1953)

### Underwear

Cotton mesh briefs and singlet – 7/6 each (1955)
Cotton rib briefs – 6/6 (1955)
Y-fronts – 6/6 (1955)
Cotton interlock briefs and singlet – 3/6 each (1955)
Cotton interlock trunks – 2/11 (1959)
Wolsey winter-weight wool & nylon trunks – 29/- (1955)
Wolsey winter-weight wool & nylon pants – 35/- (1955)

### Nightwear

Winceyette pyjamas – 25/- (1955) 19/11 (1959)
Flannelette pyjamas – 21/- (1959)
2-tone winceyette pyjamas – 25/- (1955)
Cotton pyjamas with contrasting collar & cuffs – 39/6 (1955)
Rayon dressing gown – 49/6 (1955)
Woven poplin dressing gown – 39/6 (1959)

## Clothes' Women

### Suits

Corot suit – £10.18.2 (1950)
Harella woollen suit – 8½ guineas (1952)
Debenham's suit – 32 guineas (1954)
Wooland's white wool shantung suit –19 guineas (1954)
(Harvey Nichols) Irish linen – 9½ guineas (1955)
Asta Terylene/worsted suit – 14½ guineas (1956)
All-wool suit – 15 guineas (1958)

### Coats

Women's Pakamac – from 10/6 (1953)
Corot swagger coat – £7.18.7 (1950)
Raglan Mackintosh with detachable hood – £2.16.0 (1952)
Alligator gabardine coat – £6.19.6 (1955)
Bensor fashion coat in pure worsted – 18½ guineas (1956)
Raglan tweed coat – £11.17.6 (1956)
Blue camel-hair reefer coat – 20 guineas (1954)

### Dresses & Skirts

Striped rayon short-sleeved dress – £2.5.10 (1952)
Hand-made dresses – from 5½ guineas (1955)
Hand-made cocktail dresses – from 6½ guineas (1955)
Hand-made evening gowns – from 7½ guineas (1955)
Harrods pure silk dress – 10 guineas (1955)
Everglaze cotton dress – £5.15.6 (1956)
California cotton dress – £3.19.9 (1956)
Brocade wedding dress – 13 guineas (1954)
All-wool kilt – 10 guineas (1953)
Terylene full-pleated skirt – £3.12.6 (1954)

## Various

Blouse in washable light crêpe – £4.2.6 (1953)
Robia-voile blouse with mother of pearl buttons – 3 guineas (1954)
Fine crêpe blouse in twenty-two colours – £2.5.0 (1956)
Nylon dress-style overalls – £3.9.11, OS £3.14.11 (1956)
Silk kerchief – 5/11 (1951)
Silk square – £1.9.11 (1951)
Silk scarf – £1.19.11 (1951)
Silk cravat – £1.5.9 (1954)

## Knitwear

Lambswool twin-set – £6.8.6 (1954)
Botany wool twin-set – £4.9.6 (1954)
Cashmere sweater – 7 guineas (1953)
Shetland jumpers 34 to 42 ins – £1.15.0 (1955)
Donbros fisherman knit sweater – £1.15.0 (1955)
Fair Isle gloves – 9/- pair (1952)

## Sportswear

Sports slacks – from £1.11.0 (1951)
Aertex Gladys blouse, 4in zip at neck – 15/11 (1955)
Dunlop showerproof golf jacket – £5.12.6 (1954)

## Swimwear

Flower-patterned one-piece in acetate rayon – £2.17.6 (1955)
Long-skirted, cotton one-piece – 19/11 (1955)
Hand-embroidered, boned one-piece – 11 guineas (1955)

## Underwear

Gossard bra – 5/9 (1951)
Kestos long-line bra – £1.1.11 (1955)
Twilfit nylon spot voile bra – 11/9 (1955)
Excelsior brief satin uplift bra – 3/11 (1955)
Excelsior deep bra in rayon broche – 7/9 (1955)
English Rose brief bra in sea-island cotton – 9/11 (1955)
Playtex living bra – £1.7.6, long-line £2.2.0 (1958)
Keystone panelled slip – from £1.15.11 (1955)
Keystone K-line bridal slip – from £2.6.11 (1955)
Kayser Bondor slip – from £2.5.0 (1955)
Kayser Bondor briefs – 17/9 (1955)

Rayon georgette nightie – £1.5.11 (1952)
Kayser Bondor nightdress – £3.19.11 (1955)
Wool delaine dressing gown – 6 guineas (1954)

## Foundation Garments

Gossard front-lacing corset in polka-dot broche – £3.10.1 (1951)
Kestos nylon/elastic net girdle – £2.5.0 (1955)
Twilfit girdle – £1.19.0 to £2.3.6 (1955)
English Rose pantie girdle in nylon jacquard elastic – £1.15.11 (1955)
Kempat pantie girdle – £1.12.6 (1955)
Excelsior lightly boned satin short girdle – 11/9 (1955)
Beasley's high-line rubber corset – £2.17.11 (1955)
Beasley's rubber corselette – £2.7.11 (1955)
Gossard corselette – £4.17.6 (1956)
Bayer nylon busque – £2.10.0 (1956)

## Clothes' Children

¾ hose, wool and nylon mix – 4/- to 5/8 (1954)
Ankle socks, wool and nylon mix – 2/5 to 3/3 (1954)

## Girls

Gored, double-breasted coat, velvet collar – 4 guineas (24in) to £5.1.6 (34in) (1952)
School berets – 6/3 (1955)
School blazer – 34/6 (1955)
Velour hats – 28/11 (1955)
Games tunic – 28/6 to 46/11 (1955)

## Boys

Mentor sanforised shirts – from 12/6 (1953)
School blazer – 50/- to 59/6 (1955)

## Head, Hands & Feet

## For men, women & children

Bafeez rope-soled deck shoes – 15/- pair (1955)
Bafeez espadrilles – 13/9 pair (1955)

# Men's Shoes

Bafeez fibre-soled boat shoes – 16/9 pair (1958)

# Women's Shoes

K Shoes – high-heeled suede courts – £2.17.9 leather, peep-toe £3.5.9 (1953)
Lotus, wedge-soled leather court – £3.9.9 (1953)
Clarks slimline courts – £3.15.0 (1954)
Dolcis low-cut courts – £2.9.11 to £3.9.11 (1955)
K Shoes – suede sandals – £2.15.9 kid, or patent £2.17.9 (1953)
Newman's nylon lace summer sandal – 19/- (1953)
K glacé kid sandals – £2.9.9 to £3.5.9 (1955)
Norvic sandal – high-heel – £2.19.9, flat heel £2.5.0 (1955)
K Shoes – calf casual – £3.9.9, wedge sole £2.19.9 (1953)
Lotus flat casuals, strap or lace – £3.9.9 (1955)
Liberty casuals – £2.15.0 (1955)
Church's black suede – £4.19.9 (1956)

# Children's Shoes

Boy's or girl's Gibson – £2.15.9 (1959)
Boy's or girl's bar sandal – £2.15.9 (1959)

# Stockings

Plaza 15 denier sheer – 9/11 (1955)
Plaza 12 denier sheer – 12/11 (1955)
Christian Dior – 10/6 to 18/6 (1956)
Kayser 15 denier – 11/6 (1956)
Kayser 30 denier – 9/11 (1956)

*Always look for the name*

# Hats

Tammy woman's hat in felt – 13/9 (1952)
Woman's stitched silk jersey hat – 8½ guineas (1954)
White grosgrain hat by Aage Thaarup – 15 guineas (1954)

# Gloves

Cloth gloves – 10/- (1951)
Hogskin gloves – 19/- (1951)
Suede gloves – £2.3.6 (1951)

# Accessories

## Jewellery

Bravington's 5 diamond ring – £20.0.0 (1950)
Bravington's 3 diamond ring – £9.15.0 (1950)
Cresta single diamond ring – £6.17.6 (1957)
Cresta triple diamond ring – £13.10.0 (1957)
Cresta gold signet ring – £5.0.0 (1957)
Single string pink imitation pearls – £1.10.0 (1951)

## Wedding Rings

Bravington's plain 22ct gold – £3.10.0 to £5.5.0 (1950)
Cresta gold – £4.7.6 (1957)

## Wristwatches

Kelton men's watch – £3.17.2 (1950)
Kelton ladies' watch – £4.11.6 (1950)
Men's Timex, finest leather strap – £2.7.6 (1953)
100% automatic self-winding Swiss watch – £16.16.0 (1953)
Self-winding twenty-one jewels, waterproof – £17.10.0 (1953)
Smiths five jewel – from £2.2.6 (1955)
Ladies' pure platinum-plated simulation diamond-set watch – £4.19.6 (1955)
Cyma ladies' and gents' watches – 14 guineas to £60 (1955)
Ingersoll pocket watch – £1.10.0 (1952)
Smiths pocket watch – from £1.3.9 (1955)

## Handbags

Large Laxan calf bag with gilt clasp – £8.15.0 (1954)
Bagcraft washable – £3.2.6 (1955)
Malmax bucket bag – £1.14.0 (1955)

## Cases

Pioneer tall dress pack inc. hangers – £2.19.6 (1955)
Revelation suitcase with expanding locks – £5.5.0 (1955)
Noton Gladstone case – £1.12.6 (1955)
Revelation train case – £5.9.6 (1955)
Antler small case – £3.18.6 (1955)
Pioneer round hat box – £1.19.6 (1955)
Revelation square hat box – £5.12.6 (1955)

## Umbrellas

Woman's, malacca handled – £2.17.6 (1951)
Woman's, malacca handled, nylon – £3.15.0 (1951)
Woman's slim nylon – £5.15.0 (1956)

## Material

Harris Tweed 100% wool 29in – 9/4 yard (1952–5)
Worsted tartan 54in – £2.2.0 yard (1953)
Sparva spun rayon – 4/11 yard (1958)
Sparva Tubeezy cotton – 5/11 yard (1958)

## Wool

Beehive fingering – 1/6 oz (1950)
Fair Isle fingering – 1/- oz (1950)
Beehive vest wool – 1/6 oz (1950)
Botany wool – 3 and 4 ply – 1/- oz (1952) 3 ply 1/- oz
    (1959)
Beehive sock wool – 1/3½ oz (1950)
Angora – 3/ ½ oz (1950)
Harris Double quick knit – 17/1 lb (1955)
4-ply double knitting – 1/- and 1/2 oz (1958)
Nylon double knitting – 1/8 oz (1959)
Baby wool – 1/4 oz (1950) ¼ oz (1958)

## Cosmetics & Toiletries

Grossmith 'White Fire' perfume – 9/6, 17/6 (1955)
Morny perfumes – 4/-, 12/6, 31/6 (1955)
Coty L'Aimant – 11/6 to 4 guineas (1955)
Pagan – 12/6, 22/6, 42/6, £12 (1955)
Coty Meteor – 15/6 to 8 guineas (1955)
Max Factor Primitif perfume – 8/6 (1958)
Max Factor Primitif cologne – 9/6, 15/6 (1958)
Max Factor Primitif talc – 4/4 (1958)
4711 cologne – 4/3 (1954)
Goya Black Rose cologne – 3/3 (1954–5)
Coty Twistick cologne – 7/6 (1955)
Coty talc – 4/6 (1955)
Leichner eye shadow, forty shades – 4/6, gold or silver 5/3
    (1955)
Pond's Cold Cream jars – 1/2, 2/5, 4/10 (1950) 2/3
    (1954)

Nivea cream – 1/6, 2/6, 4/9 (1952)
Coty cleansing cream – 5/3 (1955)
Elizabeth Arden cleansing cream – 8/3, 14/9, £1.2.6 (1955)
Coty cleansing milk – 6/3 (1955)
Rubinstein's Skin Clearing Cream – 5/3 (1955)
Anne French cleansing milk – 3/7 (1953)

## Foundation & Rouge

Richard Hudnut basic dew liquid foundation – 6/9 (1954)
Outdoor Girl liquid foundation – 3/9 (1958)
Max Factor Invisible foundation – 6/8 (1955)
Helena Rubinstein Silk-tone liquid rouge – 10/6 (1955)
Richard Hudnut Bloom rouge – 6/9 (1955)
Rimmel eyebrow pencil in four shades – 1/9 and 2/9 (1951)
Arancil eyebrow pencil – 3/6 (1955)

## Face Powder

Pond's – 1/2, 2/-, 3/5 (1950–1)
Goya – 3/- (1951) 5/- (1952) 4/6 (1954)
Cyclax Beauty Pressed powder – 9/9 in compact (1955)
Coty Airspun powder – 5/- (1955)
Grossmith green powder for sunburn – 4/2 (1955)
Yardley – 6/- (1958)
Yardley feather finish – 9/3 (1958)
Max Factor Pan-Cake – 4/6 (1959)

## Lipstick

Tokalon – small 1/3, large 4/10 (1950)
Cutex – 5/- (1951)
Tangee – 2/6, deluxe size 7/6, deluxe refills 3/6 (1950)
    5/-, refill 2/9 (1955)
Sans Egal indelible lipstick – 6/9, refill 3/3 (1955)
Helena Rubinstein Stay-Long lipstick – 10/6, refills 6/- (1955)
Pond's Ever So Red – 7/6 (1955)
Lip-Cote lipstick fixative – 3/2, (1951–55) 5/10 (1955)
Max Factor Red Riding Hood – 4/5 and 6/8 (1954)
Crushed Rose – 6/8 (1955)
Yardley – 6/9 (1953) 7/10 (1958) refill 3/- (1953) 4/10
    (1958)

## Nail Varnish, hand cream & hair removal

Cutex nail polish – 3/6 bottle (1951) 2/3 bottle (1955)

Helena Rubinstein Stay-Long nail lacquer – 7/6 (1955)
Revlon nail enamel – 5/3 (1955)
Snowfire hand jelly – 9d and 1/4 (1951)
Pond's Dry Skin Cream – 2/9 jar  (1952)
Cutex hand cream – tube 2/3, jar 3/6 (1959)
Veet hair removing cream – 2/2 or 3/3 (1954)

## Soap

Astral cream soap – 8½d (1950–51), 9d (1952)
Lux toilet soap – 5d, bath size 10d (1950)
Pears soap – 10½d tablet (1952)
Palmolive – 6d, bath size 10½d (1954)

## Toothpaste

Phillips Dental Magnesia – 1/4d, 2/3 (1950), 1/6, 2/3 (1954)
Maclean's Peroxide – 1/7 and 2/5 (1954)
Colgate Dental Cream – 10½d, 1/7, 2/5, 3/4 (1954)
Kolynos – 1/7 tube (1955)

## Toothbrushes

Wisdom – 1/9 (1952)

## Shampoo

Amami shampoo – 4d packet (1950)
Pears Gloria liquid shampoo – 7½d (1952)
Toni liquid shampoo – sachet 6d, bottle 3/- (1954)
Vaseline shampoo  – powder – 4½d, liquid 6d (1955)
Vosene – 1/6, 3/3 (1955)

## Home hairdressing

Estolan conditioning cream – 2/6 (1951)
Brylcreem tub – 1/8, 2/6, 4/6, tube 2/6 (1955)
Silvikrin hair cream – jar 2/9 and 3/- (1955)
Vaseline hair tonic – 2/9, 4/3 (1952) 2/6, 3/9 (1955)
Toni Home Perm spin curlers – 16/8 (1950)
Toni Home Perm standard curlers –12/6 (1950)
Toni Home Perm refill – 8/4 (1950)
Richard Hudnut Home Wave – 15/6, refill 7/- (1951), refill 9/- (1954)
Pin-Quick home perm – 9/- (1955)

Amami wave set – 1/1, 2/6 (1950) 1/4½d , 2/7½d (1953–54), 1/6, 2/9 (1959)
Snowfire wave set – 1/4, 2/4 (1954)
Tress wave set – 2/8 (1955)
Camilatone colour rinse – 8½d (1955)
Raymond aerosol hair lacquer – 12/6 (1955)
Addis beauty brushes – 12/6 (1951)
Addis beauty comb – 1/11 (1951)
Mason Pearson hair brush – 10/- to £2.12.6 (1954)
Lady Jayne slumber helmet – 2/11 to 10/6 (1951)

## At the hairdressers

Cut, shampoo and set, Vasco – 15/6 (1956)
Mayfair, shampoo and set – 8/- (1955)
Perm, restyle, shampoo and set, Vasco – £4.4.0 (1956)
The Savoy, set – 10/6 (1955)
Restyle, cut, perm, shampoo and set – 2 guineas (1955)
Mayfair, perm – 2 guineas (1955)
The Savoy, perm – 6 guineas (1955)
Machineless oil perm – 3 guineas (1955)

## Shaving soap

Erasmic stick – 3/9 (1958)
Erasmic brushless cream  – tube 2/- (1955), 2/6 (1958), jar 3/- (1955), 3/9 (1958)
Palmolive Rapid Shave aerosol, '3 months shaving in every can' – 6/6 (1955)

## Electric razors

Remington contour 6 electric – £8.10.0 (1953)
Remington 60 – £9.17.11 (1955)
Rolls Viceroy – £6.17.6 (1955)
Ronson – £8.17.6 (1955)
Philishave rotary – £7.9.3 (1955), £7.14.2 (1956), £6.16.0 to £7.11.9 (1958)

## Razors & Blades

Gillette 'Rocket' razor and six blades – 6/6 (1955)
Rolls Razor, honed and strapped in its case – £2.13.3 (1955)
Pal Injecto-Matic – 8/6 (1955)
Blue Gillette ten blades – 2/10 (1955)
Pal Injecto-Matic blades (12) – 2/9 (1955)

# The Decade of Design

**T**his was to be the jet age. The style was aero-dynamic, forward-looking, jazzy and bright. Danish designs in ceramics, furniture and cutlery were popular and influential; modern materials, formica, plastic, chrome and stainless steel prevailed. In fashion, surrealists, especially Dali, influenced some of the more modernist designers.

Two major influences on popular fashion were the music and, more importantly, film industries. Film stars had for some time been a kind of Hollywood royalty, but the link was made even firmer with the marriage of Grace Kelly to Prince Rainier of Monaco in 1956.

Marilyn Monroe had been in films since 1947, but she shot to stardom in the 1953 film **'Niagara'**. With her statuesque figure, she was the archetypal fifties woman, and was the ultimate fifties sex-symbol, and consequently fashion-aspiration. The British answer to Monroe was Diana Dors. Blonde and statuesque, she was more earthy than Marilyn, playing several girl-next-door roles. Perhaps her most famous appearance was in a mink bikini at the 1955 Venice Film Festival. The following year, the 21-year-old French actress Brigitte Bardot appeared in **'And God Created Woman'** in a skimpy bikini. She was an immediate hit and her relative youth – Marilyn was then 30 and Diana 25 – meant that she was dubbed the 'sex-kitten', and a younger, fresher look began. Her slender figure and girlish pony tail set fashion trends everywhere. Youth was also the look of Audrey Hepburn who rose to fame playing elegant gamines in films such as **'Sabrina Fair'**.

Male film stars were also influential; Tony Curtis, whose film roles throughout the fifties made him something of a heart-throb, is also one of the select group of people to have a hairstyle named after them. His version of the DA was so popular that even Elvis Presley copied it. Other influential actors included Victor Mature, Kirk Douglas and Burt Lancaster in a series of tough-guy roles.

No 33  DIANA DORS
starring in R.K.O.'s
'I Married a Woman'
PRINTED IN GREAT BRITAIN

**1950**
the trumpet coat
the sheath dress

**1951**
the trumpet skirt
October – Winston Churchill becomes Prime Minister

**1952**
February – Death of King George VI
'Florentine' stilettos first appear in America.
December – End of Utility

**1953**
January – Dwight D Eisenhower becomes President of USA
March – Stalin dies
June – Coronation of Elizabeth II
July – The USA, North Korea and China sign the armistice ending the Korean war
Stilettos arrive in Britain
Teddy boys evolve in London's East End
Film – 'The Wild One'

**1954**
the H line.
Film – 'On the Waterfront'
July – Food rationing ends

**1955**
tube dress
the A line;
Film – 'Rebel Without a Cause'
Film – 'The Blackboard Jungle'

In the field of music Elvis Presley was 'the King', but there were influential British stars including Cliff Richard, Billy Fury and Tommy Steele, all influencing the newly arrived teenage fashion world.

## Fashion Designers

Christian Dior began what would become the fifties style with the 'new look', a flamboyant, full-skirted style. This, he followed with the 'H' line, which in turn evolved into the 'A' line. Cristóbal Balenciaga took the new look and developed it, broadening the shoulders and removing the waist. In 1955, he designed the tunic dress, which developed into the chemise dress and his 1959 Empire line. Gabrielle Chanel, universally known as 'Coco', produced relaxed evening styles, and developed her 'little black dress', while Pierre Cardin resurrected the 'puff-ball' skirt, and John Cavanagh introduced 'tube' dresses and suits, and Yves Saint Laurent the wedge-shaped 'trapeze' look.

As well as working for the fashion industry, leading designers also worked with the cinema; Pierre Balmain, generally regarded as the leading French designer, designed the costumes for Brigitte Bardot's 1956 hit **'And God Created Woman'**. Hubert de Givenchy designed clothes for Audrey Hepburn in the film **'Sabrina Fair'** and went on to introduce the 'sack' dress. Antonio Castillo had been a costume designer for the New York Metropolitan Opera Company and for Broadway. In 1950, he moved to Paris to design for Lanvin, producing elegant designs on slender lines, with long flowing skirts in rich fabrics.

Most of the famous designers were, of course, based in Paris, but London had its own designers, chief among these being Hardy Amies, who became the Queen's official dressmaker in 1955, and Norman Hartnell, who had been making clothes for royalty since 1935, when he created the wedding dress for the marriage of the Duke of Gloucester, and, perhaps more importantly, the dresses for the bridesmaids, who including the then Princesses Elizabeth and Margaret. Twelve years later he was chosen by Elizabeth to design her wedding dress, and in 1953, her Coronation dress. There were also young designers starting out in London such as Jean Muir who started with Jacqmar in 1955 and joined Jaeger the following year, to specialise in knitwear design. Another newcomer, Mary Quant, set up one of London's first boutiques, 'Bazaar', on the King's Road in Chelsea in 1955.

## Bring in the New

Not all fashion innovations left their mark on history. Like the men's rubber swimming costume, or the artificial buttoneer, some never quite took off; here are just a few of them.

The fashionable look demanded an ample bosom. For those whom nature had not granted such a form, there was always cotton wool, but manufacturers helped with foam rubber and latex 'falsies'. Another device was the inflatable bra, with which, the manufacturer promised, you could add one inch to your cup by the simple method of blowing up the cup by means of a tube, long enough for the wearer to top up the bra (secretly, of course). It was not 100 per cent satisfactory, with wearers reporting leaks, sometimes accompanied by whistles and squeaks, and even balloon-like explosions.

Diana Dors would certainly not have needed such help to fill her famous mink bikini, but as a fashion accessory the mink bikini was fairly useless. Of course many bikinis never went into the sea, but I imagine it was a bit ticklish to wear, as well as being rather hot on the beach.

TIMELINE

... on Anthony Eden becomes Prime Minister

**1956**
January – Elvis Presley's first record – 'Heartbreak Hotel' released
April – the marriage of Grace Kelly to Prince Rainier of Monaco
Film – 'And God Created Woman' – Brigitte Bardot
October/November – Suez Crisis
November – Elvis Presley's first film – 'Love me Tender' released

**1957**
January – Harold MacMillan becomes Prime Minister
January – Tommy Steele tops hit parade with 'Singing the Blues'
July – MacMillan makes his 'Britons "have never had it so good"' speech
the sack dress.
The spindle line

**1958**
Trapeze dress
The hula hoop
August – Cliff Richard's first record, 'Move It', released

**1959**
October – The Conservatives under MacMillan win General election

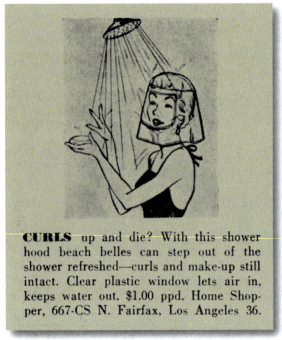

CURLS up and die? With this shower hood beach belles can step out of the shower refreshed—curls and make-up still intact. Clear plastic window lets air in, keeps water out. $1.00 ppd. Home Shopper, 667-CS N. Fairfax, Los Angeles 36.

Then there was the car hat rack, fitted to the inside roof of a saloon car: *'the Antennial holds hat firmly upside down, out of the way. Well made of chromium plated brass, arms covered in flexible plastic. Price 15s 6d.'*

Throughout the fifties men's fashion designers struggled to introduce the kinds of design innovations into their clothes which the female fashion world revelled in. The whole Teddy-boy look had sprung from just such an ill-fated venture. Another occurred in 1958, when Yves Saint Laurent introduced the wedge-shaped 'trapeze' dress for women. In Britain, designers of the 'Men's Fashion Council' tried to extend the fashion into men's clothes, calling it 'Trapeze-Line Tailoring or Fashion with a Flare'. E. H. Watson, Chairman of the Council and tailor to the Duke of Edinburgh, described the look; *'the jackets and coats flare prominently at the back with the sleeves in both cases curving outwards at the cuffs'* – these were called 'Musketeer cuffs' – *'The trousers, which are almost bell-bottomed in the naval tradition, are also flared and finished without turn-ups. The Trapeze line has been incorporated into topcoats, dress suits, town and country suits, and casual jackets.'* Needless to say it did not get very far.

## Man-made fibres

This was the decade of synthetic fibre. Nylon had first been produced commercially in 1938, but it reached its heyday in the fifties, with variations such as socks in wool and nylon mixtures. *'Nylon hosiery for men nowadays means stretch nylon socks for all shapes and sizes of feet, bulked nylon and Ban-Lon nylon. The Ban-Lon process for nylon, so successful for underwear, has now resulted in new ranges of socks from hosiery manufacturers.'* Ban-Lon was a trademark used for knitted and woven fabrics made from artificially crimped yarns. There were 'Shirts in Taslan-textured nylon', and Perlon, a filmy, opaque nylon much used for underwear.

Then there was Terylene, a synthetic polyester fibre, and the first wholly synthetic fibre invented in Britain, in 1941. The following year the rights had been sold to ICI and bulk production began in 1955. Soon after it was being used in a 65 per cent wool, 35 per cent Terylene blend for suits. By 1958, **Men Only** was writing that 'Now that Terylene is being used for men's knitwear – one of its most recent applications – there's hardly anything that a man wears, from his hat to his socks, that is not being made up, in this versatile polyester fibre. Hats, ties, shirts, underwear, socks, topcoats, raincoats, suits and slacks, dress wear; you can have them all in Terylene.' There was also 100 per cent Terylene Ban-Lon. *'It will not shrink or lose its shape with constant washing'*, or *'an uncrushable, unharmable hat made from a mixture of Terylene and fur'*.

Originally known as 'Fibre A' by its inventors DuPont, Orlon, an acrylic fibre, began to be produced commercially in 1950, while production in the UK began in 1959 under the names of 'Courtelle' and 'Acrilan': 'Bulky-knit sweater and socks in 100% Orlon'. By 1958 *'Acrilan and worsted and Acrilan wool suits are in most manufacturers' ranges. Acrilan is also being developed for knitwear. One of its latest applications in the men's trade is for scarves.'* There were also shirts available in half cotton and half Courtelle, which was *'the new British acrylic fibre introduced by Courtaulds'*.

*Men's Trapeze-line suit, 1958.*

# Bibliography

## Books

Caldwell, Doreen – *And all was revealed* – pub. Arthur Baker Ltd. 1981
Clancy, Deirdre – *Costume since 1945* – pub. Herbert Press 1996
Constantino, Maria – *Men's Fashion in the 20th Century* – pub. Batsford 1997
Ewing, Elizabeth – *History of 20th Century Fashion* – pub. Batsford 1974
Harris, Carol – *Collecting Fashion and Accessories* – pub. Miller's 2000
*Utility Fashion and Furniture 1941 – 1951* – pub. ILEA 1974

## Pamphlets, etc.

*Glorify Yourself* – The Academy of Charm and Beauty

## Periodicals

Blighty
Dioptric News
Everywoman
Illustrated
London Life
Men Only
Needlecraft & Needlewoman
Picture Post
Stitchcraft
The Tatler
True Story
Wide World Magazine
Woman's Companion
Woman's Day
Woman's Own
Woman's Realm
Woman's Weekly
Vogue

# INDEX

The 1950s Look